Leading
Congregational
Change

Leading Congregational Change

A Practical Guide for the
Transformational Journey

Jim Herrington
Mike Bonem
James H. Furr

Jossey-Bass Publishers • San Francisco

Jossey-Bass books and products are available through most bookstores. To contact Jossey-Bass directly, call (888) 378–2537, fax to (800) 605–2665, or visit our website at www.josseybass.com.

Substantial discounts on bulk quantities of Jossey-Bass books are available to corporations, professional associations, and other organizations. For details and discount information, contact the special sales department at Jossey-Bass.

Library of Congress Cataloging-in-Publication Data

Herrington, Jim, date
  Leading congregational change : a practical guide for the transformational journey / Jim Herrington, Mike Bonem, and James Furr. — 1st ed.
    p. cm.
  Includes bibliographical references and index.
  ISBN 0-7879-4765-2 (alk. paper)
    1. Church growth. I. Bonem, Mike, date II. Furr, James, date III. Title
BV652.25 .H47 2000
253—dc21   99-006924

HB Printing   10 9 8 7 6 5 4 3 2   FIRST EDITION

Contents

996.24

Preface

"If you keep doing what you've been doing, you'll keep getting what you've been getting." We use this expression frequently in seminars on congregational change, because we believe that the call for transformation is clear and emphatic. The Scripture says, "Do not conform any longer to the pattern of this world, but be *transformed* by the renewing of your mind" (Romans 12:2). God offers personal transformation as we ✈ enter into relationship with him. He also wants to transform our congregations. We believe that the call for congregational transformation is just as clear and just as urgent.

Why do today's congregations need to be "transformed"? Is something wrong if a church takes care of its members and maintains stable attendance while preserving its traditions? Traditions and rituals have a great value, and effective care ministries are always needed. But Christ established his church to proclaim and demonstrate salvation to the world. The call of the Great Commission is just as relevant and urgent today as it was when Jesus gave it to his disciples. Our assertion is that a healthy church will have a holistic understanding of the Gospel and that it will be reaching people for Christ at the same time that it is discipling and ministering to its members.

A Pattern of Decline

The state of Christianity in America provides ample evidence that we "keep doing what we've been doing." As churches and denominations rode the baby boom wave of growth and prosperity in the 1950s and 1960s, we became smugly confident that we "had all the answers." In the

1970s, we were too busy running our successful programs to see the shifts in our society and to understand their deep implications. When growth tapered off and decline set in, we were convinced that it was a temporary problem. Or we blamed any number of uncontrollable, external factors while clinging to our "tried-and-true" ways.

The facts paint a stark picture of the results of this approach. The portion of the population that is active in congregational life is decreasing, as is Christianity's moral influence in our culture. Approximately two-thirds of the Protestant congregations in America have long-term attendance trends that are either flat or declining. This book is not a statistical study of the state of the church, nor do we believe that faith can be expressed as a mathematical formula. We do believe that a church will grow when it understands and is genuinely committed to the biblical principle of demonstrating and sharing the Gospel in relevant ways. Growth will be manifested as internal strength, measured by the deeper commitment levels of its members. And it will have an external dimension, as more people in the community hear God's call and become faithful disciples of Christ.

Some congregations see a pattern of decline or of limited effectiveness in reaching their community, but are convinced that they are on the verge of "turning a corner." All too often this is just wishful thinking. They might make minor incremental adjustments and experience a brief upturn before the underlying pattern of decline resumes. This mindset is frequently the justification for not making more difficult and dramatic changes. These congregations are recognized by mantras like, "Don't fix something that's not broken," "We've got those problems behind us," and "Let's see how this one change plays out." Then another year passes and things are much the same as before.

Many pastors and other church leaders readily recognize this pattern. George Barna, Bill Easum, Kennon Callahan, and others have described the struggles and characteristics of the modern church in detail. Thousands of pastors and key leaders attend conferences every year in search of the latest "quick-fix" answers. The real issue, though, is not whether change is needed or even whether models of faithful and effective churches exist today. Congregational leaders know the current state of the church and can envision the power of a reenergized, vibrant congregation. The question is how to transform a fifty-year-old congregation—with all of its traditions, rules, and patterns—from the former to the latter. How does a pastor deal with resistance from key members who do not understand why change is needed? How should God's vision for the congregation be discerned and implemented? What are the pitfalls and risks to be avoided? These are the kinds of issues that are critical to transformation and that this book addresses.

An Opportunity to Share

We write this book out of a deep conviction that bold transformation is needed in many of the congregations that cover the American landscape. We believe that the face of our society in the future will be radically different if some portion of these congregations begins making real progress toward God's vision for their ministries. The investments made by our predecessors and the destiny of future generations are too important not to take transformation seriously.

We also write out of a sense of obedience. After working with many different congregations and congregational leaders, it is clear that practical resources on congregational transformation are needed. Our fifty-plus years of combined experience includes staff positions in local churches, denominational work focused on assisting individual churches, business and congregational consulting, and leadership development in conference settings. In much of this experience, transformation has been an explicit or underlying theme. We also bring a deep commitment to the biblical role of the local church. Our common affiliation with Union Baptist Association in Houston has been an enormous opportunity to work together in a "living laboratory." As we learned and adapted many innovative tools, we recognized the uniqueness of the perspective and contribution that we offer.

The framework and principles of change that are presented in this book are not untested hypotheses. Our learning has come from working with over a hundred highly diverse congregations that are dealing with transformational issues, and from teaching the change process in interactive settings to over a thousand pastors, staff members, and lay leaders. Over time, we have distilled our experience into the simple, memorable, and transferable concepts on which this book is based.

Our learning also comes from reading the work of a variety of Christian and secular writers. Our belief and experience is that congregations and secular organizations share many characteristics. Consequently, insights from the broader study of organizations can often be applied in some manner to congregations. The concepts in this book have been examined in light of our own theological and ecclesiological convictions. We also tested their validity in our consultations with individual congregations. The resulting description of congregational transformation is richer because of the broad knowledge base that it reflects.

A Framework for Transformation

In developing this material, we have focused on principles and concepts, not on narrowly defined "how to" prescriptions. This allows application across a broad spectrum of congregations. We emphasize the practical and concrete, not the theoretical and abstract.

This book is designed primarily for pastors and other congregational leaders who sense that things are not "just fine" in their churches and realize that deep change is needed. Judicatory staff and church consultants who are providing assistance to these congregations will also find the model for congregational transformation helpful. Along with the accompanying workbook, our intent is to provide a resource that will be practical and useful throughout the transformational journey.

Even though most of the examples in the pages that follow focus on transformation of established congregations, this book has other applications. Individual ministries within a congregation can use it to facilitate their own transformation. The key leadership disciplines and the steps for developing commitment are just as applicable to a new congregation as to a hundred-year-old church. Parachurch organizations will also deal with many of the same issues and challenges.

Regardless of their individual role or their specific context, we encourage readers to be adaptive and critical as they consider this material. Personal application will bring the concepts to life and make the book more useful. We present principles for change, not rigid formulas. The key concepts of congregational transformation—such as God's call for transformation, the central role of spiritual vitality, the sequential nature of effective change, and the learning disciplines—are essential and universal. The illustrations and action items are offered as suggestions and starting points for discussion. Congregational leaders should adapt these to fit the needs, personality, and history of their own congregations. If an idea does not fit your church's theology, polity, or heritage, then modify or replace it with an approach that leads to the same or better result. Even the process of asking how to apply the principles of transformation within a congregation can be a major step forward.

Chapter One introduces and describes the development of the Congregational Transformation Model. This model is the framework that we use to explain and guide change processes in congregations. The chapters that follow examine each piece of the model in greater detail. Although the chapters follow a logical progression, readers will find it easy to skip to the topics that are of greatest interest or relevance to their needs.

Each chapter includes a combination of descriptive information, illustrations, and suggestions for leading transformation. Although we have used fictional names in the case histories, the stories are taken from actual experiences. For leaders who want to guide their congregations through transformation, the companion workbook goes into greater detail on the "how to" questions. It contains a number of individual and group exercises that are based on the Congregational Transformation Model.

To the pastors who will read this book, we offer our heartfelt gratitude and admiration. Those who have recognized the need for transformation know that they face many challenges. The tension of feeling a clear call from God but confronting the complexity of transformation can be overwhelming. We find inspiration in a growing number of positive stories about revitalized congregations and in Christ's assurance that "everything is possible for him who believes" (Mark 9:23).

In *Deep Change*, Robert Quinn (1996) asserts that organizations tend to lose focus on their mission and to become stagnant over time. As this happens, they must make a conscious decision to change. If they do not, they will continue down a path of decline. He refers to this as the "deep change or slow death dilemma" (p. 16). But Quinn does not stop with the organization. He maintains that successful change leaders realize that the problem is not "out there," but that deep change must begin at a personal level.

And so an underlying theme of this book is that congregational transformation is essential, but it will only occur when leaders commit to personal transformation. Personal transformation has a very real cost, but so does failure to change. The expression at the beginning of this chapter was actually incomplete. In its entirety, it is not a statement but a question for all leaders to ponder: "If you keep doing what you've been doing, you'll keep getting what you've been getting. *Can you live with that?*"

December 1999
Jim Herrington
Houston, Texas

Mike Bonem
Bellaire, Texas

James H. Furr
Houston, Texas

For our parents

Jim and Helen Herrington
Joe and Diane Bonem
Jack and June Furr

from whom we first learned
to love the church
with all our
hearts and minds and souls

Acknowledgments

Writing this book has truly been a team learning experience. Each of us brought particular emphases and specialties to the process. We began by writing out of our strengths. Our individual work was brought to the team, which then shaped, changed, and strengthened what was offered. Hundreds of conversations—sometimes conflicted, other times seeming to sweep us beyond the moment to new awareness and personal learning—undergird this work.

We have learned from far too many teachers to mention them all. We are deeply grateful to the team that provided the context of our learning. More than work colleagues, these folks are our friends. This book is a reflection of the learning that happened among us. The contributions of Tom Billings, Rickie Bradshaw, Mary Ann Bridgwater, Michael Cox, Robert Creech, Al Guerra, Sally Hinzie, Dian Kidd, Bill Lewey, Rick Ogden, Ken Shuman, Karen Simon, Robert Sowell, and Ron Towery are on every page of this book. We are also indebted to the pastors and congregations of Union Baptist Association. In these congregations, we were allowed to teach and learn. The material in these pages has been refined over and over by what we learned from them.

We thank Rick Warren and Doug Slaybaugh for the opportunity to teach and refine our understanding of congregational transformation as part of Saddleback Valley Church's Purpose-Driven Church Conference. We are also grateful to Bob Buford, Carol Childress, Dave Travis, and others at Leadership Network for the many ways in which they have stimulated and facilitated our work.

Finally, we thank our families. Betty Herrington, Bonnie Bonem, and Rhonda Furr love us, release us to ministry, believe the best in us, and encourage us on. Especially in the final days of preparing the manuscript, their patience and understanding were invaluable.

This book is a labor of love, in the purest sense of the word. All three of us are deeply committed to the local congregation. We've all had experiences providing leadership for congregations that were struggling to find the pathway to change. We've all suffered the pain of failure, and we've experienced the joy of success. It is for the pastors and leaders of congregations seeking to follow God's transformational leadership that we have written this book.

J. H.

M. B.

J. H. F.

Leading Congregational Change

Chapter 1

Learning to Lead Change

A Transformational Journey

MANY CHRISTIAN CONGREGATIONS in America today need to experience life-giving transformation. If the need is so compelling, why are these congregations not embracing and initiating change? In fact, many have attempted to make adjustments. But their efforts often run into resistance or produce marginal results. When this happens, they may conclude that "we can't change—we'll just have to make the best of it."

There's good news! God is still eager and able to re-create both people and congregations. Furthermore, the principles of leading transformation can be learned by most church leaders in ordinary congregations.

Over the past decade, a group of churches in Houston, Texas, has passionately engaged the question, "How do we transform declining congregations into Christ-like bodies that display the power of the Gospel in our communities?" Today congregations everywhere are struggling with the rapid-fire changes in our world and the impact these changes are having on their ministries. How do churches respond to these changes and remain true to the core teachings of the Scripture?

These are questions that the churches of Union Baptist Association (UBA) have been addressing for more than a decade. This book presents the model and principles for congregational transformation that emerged from their journey. In sharing the lessons from our experience, we hope to encourage other congregations and to help them navigate their own tumultuous environments.

In this chapter, we relate the story of the model's development in UBA. The story actually unfolds on two levels—the transformation of a local judicatory and of many individual congregations. With the benefit of hindsight, we are able to tell the story in an orderly fashion. As we lived it, the actual experience was anything but orderly. Fueled by a passion for the local church, pastors and judicatory leaders prayed, studied, dialogued, and experimented. We learned as much from our failures as we did from our successes. We experienced conflict at many different levels. The process was both humbling and rewarding, two emotions that any change leader will ultimately experience.

How successful has the journey been? In the 1980s, Southern Baptist congregations lost ground, when compared to the overall growth of the population, in every county in the country. From 1990 to 1995, the Southern Baptist churches in Houston grew by 19.2 percent while the county grew by an estimated 12.9 percent. Baptisms increased by nearly 50 percent, and giving to the association increased dramatically. A clear and compelling vision is shared among this group of denominational churches in a day that proclaims the death of denominational loyalties. This book is not about denominational revitalization, but we do advocate that congregational leaders learn and draw support from others to navigate the waters of change successfully.

The church in America is at a crossroads. We share our story to offer hope to churches across the country—hope in a practical, proven process that can help create a renewed sense of vitality and impact. Though it is written by three church consultants, this is the story of courageous pastors and congregational leaders who allowed us to learn with them as they embraced the journey of change.

Two Defining Moments: Catalysts for Change

Our story begins in the fall of 1989. The UBA staff team experienced two clarifying moments that set the course for a decade of learning about change leadership. The previous spring, I (Jim Herrington) was called to serve as the director of this association of five hundred Southern Baptist churches in the Houston area. The two colleagues who coauthor this book joined the team almost immediately. James Furr became a member of the staff team, serving as a consultant to local congregations. Mike Bonem served as my personal consultant in the effort to clarify UBA's mission and vision for the future.

A Fresh Look at the Trends

The first defining moment grew out of a statistical analysis. James profiled the membership, attendance, and giving trends for all our churches as a group from 1950 through 1989. The graphs reflected generally positive growth in all the categories. My immediate response to this picture was "This looks good. We've done well over the past forty years."

Then James finished the story. On top of the trend lines for the association, he laid a graph of the growth of the city for the same period. The message was startling. It showed a gap between the growth of the churches and the growth of the city that grew wider every year. In business terms, we had been losing market share for forty years. At the annual meeting of our churches each fall, we would congratulate ourselves for an increase in resident membership, while failing to acknowledge that the city had grown significantly faster during the same year. We had actually lost ground. With few exceptions, this pattern had repeated itself for forty years.

Feedback from the Front Lines

Determined to discover the causes of this trend, we convened a series of seventeen listening sessions with pastors around the city. This produced the second defining moment. A total of 176 pastors participated. They represented congregations of all sizes, of the inner city and the suburbs, and of eight different cultures.

On a Tuesday night in September 1989, we convened a listening session at Faith Memorial Baptist Church. Sixteen pastors attended, and several brought their spouses. As the meeting unfolded, a pastor named Dave decided to give us some painfully honest feedback. "I never open any mail that comes from the denomination. You guys don't have a clue what my world is like. You keep sending me standardized programs with promises that my church will successfully reach the community, if I just use the program the way you designed it. When I say that it's not working, you tell me that I'm either doing something wrong or that I'm not working hard enough."

He paused and looked at the floor. When he looked up again, there were tears in his eyes. "I'm working harder than I've ever worked, for less results than I've ever gotten. My health is failing and my family is falling apart. And I feel abandoned by my denomination. I want nothing more than to see my community embrace the Gospel. But one thing is clear to me. Working harder at what we've been doing is simply not the answer."

That night we gathered around Dave and prayed for him. I thanked him for the courage to be honest. Then came the clarifying moment. I looked at the other pastors and said, "It would help me to know how much Dave's experiences mirror your own."

We did not leave the room until after midnight. These men and women poured out hearts of frustration and confusion. They knew, long before we did a statistical analysis, that we were losing the city. They knew that their best efforts were not producing the results that they desired and that their communities needed. They were brokenhearted over the lack of impact their churches were having. And they were frustrated that their training had not prepared them for this world. It was clear that they were looking for credible guides to share the risks of navigating this new world, and none were to be found.

As I drove home that night, I found myself talking out loud to God. I asked him for wisdom. I made a promise that if he would show the way to help pastors and congregations have an impact on our city, I would follow no matter what the cost. At that time I had no way of knowing the full significance of this covenant. In retrospect, I wonder if I would have been so quick to make that promise had I realized what was ahead. I did not understand the power of a paradigm. I could not foresee the resistance to change that would come. I did not anticipate the personal attacks or the sense of abandonment that I would feel at various points along the way. I now know that these are common experiences for every change leader. As I began the journey, the cliché, "ignorance is bliss" contained more than a grain of truth.

Changing Our Association Before We Could Help Others

These two defining moments produced a sense of urgency that drove us to prayer, to dialogue, and to a commitment to learn. (See Chapter Three about the role of creating urgency in successful change processes.) We readily acknowledged that we were guilty of offering only standardized, denominational programs. And it was clear that the results of these programs were overwhelmed by the scope of the need in our city. The only conclusion was that the association would need to make radical changes.

But not everyone in the organization agreed. Despite compelling evidence, many pastors and UBA staff members still wanted us to hold tightly to the traditional ways. For nearly two years, we ran on two, parallel tracks. On one track we continued offering standard denominational programs and support.

It was from the other track that the new vision ultimately emerged. This was the track of generative learning—of seeking new solutions to the challenges we faced. It only became a "track" in retrospect. In the midst of the moment, it felt more like fighting our way through a dense, deeply forested jungle. We continued listening to pastors, building relationships with them, and earning their trust.

We also found Henry Blackaby and Claude King's *Experiencing God* to be very helpful. The authors describe that God is always at work around us, and that he invites us to become involved with him in his work (1990, pp. 19–20). (See Chapter Five on the ongoing challenge of alignment.) We began to take small groups of pastors away for one-day prayer retreats. We prayed for God to show us his activity in our world. We made covenants with him and with each other that we would make adjustments to join God as his activity became clear. (See Chapter Two on spiritual vitality and Chapter Three on personal preparation.)

We read extensively from both Christian and business literature about healthy, effective organizations. We were deeply influenced by Bill Hybels and Rick Warren and the successes of their congregations. We also saw many applications in Peter Senge's *The Fifth Discipline* (1990) and in John Kotter's *Leading Change* (1996).

As the process continued, a vision for the future began to emerge and gain clarity. The vision had its roots in our very first feeble attempt at drafting a vision statement for the organization. (See Chapter Four on discerning vision.) Over time that vision became clearer and ultimately was expressed this way:

> UBA's vision is healthy congregations changing
> the world from the inside out.

This was a very stressful period. Our staff team was composed of highly competent professionals who set high standards and were accustomed to knowing the answers. Our own image of leadership made it difficult to be in the role of learner. There is a certain vulnerability that comes from acknowledging that we don't know what we need to know to succeed. Yet in today's rapidly changing environment, leaders are increasingly required to be learners.

We also experienced resistance to change from those who were primarily involved in the association's ongoing services. As the vision gained clarity, we began to ask what changes we needed to make. This created an increasing level of anxiety among those who were committed to our traditional track. This anxiety was expressed in hundreds of different conversations and decisions along the way.

Our stress was compounded by the absence of an adequate process for leading change. Our collective experiences were with incremental approaches to change. Only in retrospect did we realize that we were engaged in a *paradigm shift*. (See Chapter Eight on mental models.) We operated more from intuition and from a willingness to risk failure in order to learn. And we were sustained by a deep commitment to Jesus Christ and a conviction that change was absolutely necessary.

Understanding the Dynamics of Change

The pursuit of God's vision for UBA led us first to assess the planning processes that congregations were using. At that time, our denomination used a long-range planning process that was based on a set of standard programs. Churches assessed the strength of their existing programs, without ever asking whether these were the right programs. They followed this assessment by setting goals for increased participation in each area. The message from our pastors, however, was that standardized programming was no longer effective.

Emergence of the First Part of the Model

In the spring of 1991, UBA team member Robert Sowell initiated a pilot project to test the impact of a different planning process. This strategic planning process differed from long-range planning in several critical ways. (The planning process for change that ultimately emerged is described in Chapters Three through Five.) Ideally, it began with a thorough assessment that included internal measures—attendance, giving, membership. But it also required congregations to assess external factors, such as demographic trends and community needs.

Second, the strategic planning process included the development of a mission and vision statement that congregations could use to guide and assess their progress. Rather than measure progress against itself (did our attendance increase compared to last year?), the congregation would begin to measure progress by its impact on the community.

Third, it guided congregations to identify the key priorities that would enable them to make the most progress toward achieving their mission and vision. These priorities became the focus of new activity in the life of the church.

Ten congregations enlisted in the pilot project. The pastors of these congregations participated in a two-day retreat where the strategic planning process was described. We offered to serve as consultants to the churches as they engaged in this planning process. All ten pastors signed on for the project.

Only one of the congregations in the pilot project had a highly successful experience. Hoi Thanh Tin Lanh Baptist Vietnam, pastored by Khanh Huynh, experienced significant long-term growth. From a congregation of approximately forty members, it is now a healthy, vibrant congregation with an average attendance of three hundred fifty that is making a significant impact in the Vietnamese community of Houston and beyond.

In every other congregation that seriously engaged the process, a common pattern emerged. The strategic planning process began with great enthusiasm. The congregation developed a clearer sense of its situation and its environment and eventually established a vision. Then as the vision-based priorities were implemented, significant conflict emerged.

Learning from Conflict

In retrospect, this conflict should not have been surprising. It paralleled what was happening in our association. As we used the strategic planning process and pursued the vision for the association, the old ways of doing things were challenged. This resulted in an accelerating level of conflict. As new financial resources became available, they were budgeted, almost exclusively, to the new priorities identified in our planning. This threatened those who had a vested interest in the way we had always done things. We experienced passive and direct resistance from some staff members and from pastors in the association. Usually the conflict was behind the scenes, but more than once our deployment of resources to the new priorities was challenged in open meetings.

Over time and through hundreds of conversations we came to recognize that change does not happen without conflict. As we reviewed the biblical patterns, every time—without exception—the people of God began to make adjustments to join God in his activity, conflict emerged. Blackaby and King (1990) call it "the crisis of belief."

I would like to say that the conflict was civil and was conducted at the philosophical level. Often it wasn't. In the midst of change, the best and the worst of human nature emerges. On many occasions, the conflict became very personal. Our motives and character were questioned and challenged many times. Sometimes in the heat of the conflict, our motives were indeed suspect. On more than one occasion, we contributed to the destructive nature of these confrontations.

How did we survive this as an association? Ultimately the answer is "By the grace of God." But many factors contributed. At the core of the change process was a staff team and a group of key pastoral leaders who were deeply committed to joining God's movement. They possessed high levels of interpersonal skills that helped us manage conflict constructively. Our broadly shared sense that we were losing the city resulted in a high level of urgency. This urgency created an unusual willingness to take risks and explore new alternatives.

In our pilot project with the ten congregations, we had assumed that they had the resources needed to manage conflict. In fact, it became clear that one of the prevailing assumptions, or mental models (see Chapter Eight), was that a healthy congregation did not have conflict. As one pastor said, "All my life, I've judged my success by how happy everyone in the church was. You are telling me that if I'm really on mission with God, one sign of my success will be the presence of conflict."

The conflict in the local church was similar in content and scope to our experience at the associational level. Change threatened those individuals within the congregation who had a deep commitment to and vested interest in the existing programs and priorities. Their response to this threat varied from reasoned conversation to personal attack. As this pattern emerged in multiple congregations, it became apparent that conflict management skills would be critical to any successful change process.

Emergence of the Second Part of the Model

Heavily influenced by Blackaby and King, we began to refer to strategic planning as the work a congregation does to (1) identify the activity of God and (2) make the personal and congregational adjustments needed to join him in that activity. As we framed it in that language, the second part of our transformation model began to emerge.

In follow-ups with the ten pilot congregations and in ongoing work with many other congregations, we learned that conflict emerged in each case. The conversations gave birth to the distinction between life-giving conflict and life-threatening conflict.

Life-threatening conflict occurs when people lose sight of the vision to which God has called them. It is found in the Exodus story. After leaving Egypt for the Promised Land, the people lost sight of the mission. They began to murmur against their leadership and they openly disobeyed God. They became more concerned with their own comfort than with achievement of God's plan.

Life-giving conflict is a deeper understanding and commitment that grows out of a significant disagreement. It is found in Acts 6. In this passage, a conflict emerges over distribution of food to the widows. But as the church genuinely seeks God's will in the context of its vision, a better solution is found and the church is able to carry out its mission more effectively.

Khanh Huynh verified that the process created conflict in the Hoi Thanh congregation. "We lost members because we made a commitment to do what we understood God to be calling us to do. Some people did not want to go where God was leading us. Ultimately some people left our church. But even in losing members we became a stronger, more focused congregation."

We began to understand that a congregation must have a certain foundation before making the adjustments that the planning process will require. We refer to this foundation as spiritual and relational vitality (see Chapter Two). The change process, by its very nature, creates conflict. A congregation with a high level of spiritual and relational vitality can accept change and can manage conflict in ways that give life. Conversely, a congregation with a low level of spiritual and relational vitality will tend to manage conflict in ways that preserve the status quo.

The ways in which spiritually mature leaders manage conflict can help stimulate the change process. Though leaders and followers can and must learn skills to manage conflict, this is more an art than a science. As leaders assess the sources of conflict, they will also give attention to managing the conflict in a life-giving manner. This requires patience, wisdom, and a multitude of counselors. It requires a great deal of humility, because sometimes the leader's own broken humanity will be the source of the conflict. How a congregation manages conflict can enhance or diminish the congregation's spiritual and relational vitality. When managed in a life-giving manner, conflict empowers the people to solve the problem and keep the church on mission.

Again, this paralleled our experience in UBA. At times, the conflict was life-threatening. In other instances, conflict produced a renewed commitment to the vision and clarity in our immediate direction. In looking back, our level of spiritual and relational vitality was an important factor that separated the two outcomes. Some of our most significant advances grew out of periods when we intentionally focused on God and when relationships among our core group were strongest.

At the core of the spiritual and relational vitality part of our model is the conviction that leaders bear a disproportionate share of the responsibility for leading change. It follows that the spiritual and relational vitality of the leader or leaders is foundational to the change journey.

One additional learning emerged from our pilot project. It became clear that spiritual and relational vitality had to be linked to a positive vision of the future. In the context of this awareness, the importance of mental models (see Chapter Eight) emerged again.

Most church members have a set of assumptions about how the congregation should function. It was at this point that we learned that spiritual and relational vitality can be misplaced. The assumptions about the congregation may not be appropriate for the congregation's current context. As a congregation gives attention to increasing its vitality, one result can be an attempt to recapture the past. Several of the congregations involved in the pilot project had reached their peak in attendance a decade or more prior to this project. As pastors became intentional about fostering growth in the spiritual and relational vitality of the congregation, many of the longtime members wanted to focus that energy on recapturing the past—returning to the good old days.

As the journey continued to unfold, we began to work with congregational leaders to assess their spiritual vitality. Emphasis was given to leading the congregation to prepare for the journey of change—corporately through worship, reconciliation, and community assessment, and individually through the practice of spiritual disciplines and obedience to the Spirit's leading.

Spiritual and relational vitality emerged as the second part of our model for leading change. But it is the foundational piece. Apart from a strong sense of vitality—in relationship to God and with one another through a shared vision—the change process is doomed to failure.

Learning Why the Change Process Stalled: The Third Part of the Model

Five years into this journey, numerous congregations had embraced the change process with spiritual and relational vitality at its core. Working with consultants from the UBA team, congregations began to make progress—incremental at first, but more substantial over time. Then the final piece of learning emerged.

When the consultants exited, the process often stalled. Ultimately, the business community helped us understand the cause. Led by the work of Bennis and Nanus in the 1980s, business experts began to make a distinction between leadership and management. "Managers are people who do things right and leaders are people who do the right things" (1985, p. 21). This resonated with our experience. Most of the pastors with whom we worked had been trained to *manage* the congregation. They approached their work from the question "How do I improve the programs and ministries that we are currently doing?" Few had been trained to ask the question "Are the things we are doing the most faithful and effective means of reaching our community with the Gospel?"

It became increasingly apparent that the consultants had been virtually *leading* the change process, with the pastor endorsing it, empowering it, and continuing to manage the existing programs and ministries of the church. To achieve the vision, pastors and key congregational leaders needed a way to distinguish the leading and managing functions— but based on a paradigm of rapid change and continuous learning.

The work of Peter Senge in *The Fifth Discipline* became profoundly influential at this point. He describes leadership as mastering a set of disciplines that leaders must use to guide an organization through turbulent times. The associational team had read his work in the early 1990s and began using these disciplines in their work. Hence, the third portion of the model emerged.

Coming to terms with the learning aspects of transformational leadership had two specific impacts in our work at UBA. At the associational level, we gave birth to the Director Team. This team consists of four individuals who serve as co-directors of the association. The fundamental tenet of this approach is an agreement that no directional decisions are made without the consensus of each team member. This team allowed us to benefit from very different gifts and significantly different styles in the leadership of the association.

Our learning on leadership also led to the birth of a significant ministry named Young Leaders. Recognizing that most pastors had been trained to manage a congregation, Young Leaders became the place where we began training them to exercise transformational leadership. The program includes the content of this book and is based on a commitment to learn leadership in the context of community. Beyond the content, this two-year learning process includes very close and at times deeply challenging peer-group experiences. The participants have consistently reported that this is the most successful leadership development experience that they have ever encountered.

The final aspect of the model focuses on the cluster of learning disciplines that must be mastered by transformational leaders. The disciplines assume an environment of rapid change and significant diversity. They are substantively different from the skills required to manage the ongoing life of a congregation where little change is anticipated.

The Congregational Transformation Model

The Congregational Transformation Model, which emerged from the experiences we've described, is shown in Figure 1.1. This model was designed to describe a complex set of challenges, steps, and leadership requirements that are associated with a deep, systemic change effort in an established congregation. The principles on which the model is based are also applicable to a new church start-up, a ministry within a church, judicatories, and parachurch organizations. The model has three major interdependent and interactive components: spiritual and relational vitality, an eight-stage process for change, and four essential learning disciplines. Each component is introduced in this chapter and explained in detail in the chapters that follow.

Spiritual and relational vitality forms the heart of the transformation process. Congregations without an adequate level of vitality will not be able to sustain significant change. A congregation that is not committed to following God or that is experiencing serious discord within the body will find it virtually impossible to follow the difficult path of transformation (see Chapter Two).

The eight-stage change process is the sequential component of the model that gives form and direction to the transformation. It is not enough to know that change is needed, or even to have a clear image of the church's future. The challenge is to create a realistic way to get there. The eight stages give structure and sequence to the process of moving from today's reality to a distant tomorrow (see Chapters Three through Five).

The third component represents a set of learning disciplines that are essential for the leaders who will guide the transformation. Without these disciplines, the many hurdles that are encountered in the long journey are probably insurmountable (see Chapters Six through Ten).

When asked how long it takes to transform a congregation, we always reply that there is no simple answer. The transformation of an existing congregation is never a quick or easy process. The actual time required will depend on many factors, including the scale of the change

FIGURE 1.1   Congregational Transformation Model

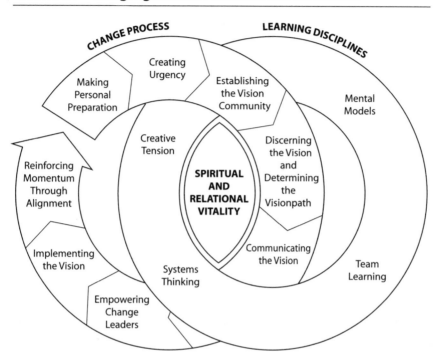

needed, church size, the congregation's readiness to transform, its spiritual and relational vitality, and past problems that may have been mishandled. Likewise, various stages in the change process will take differing amounts of time.

But a realistic figure for comprehensive transformation might be five to seven years, or sometimes longer. By comprehensive we mean deep changes such as a shift to ministries that target unchurched persons, a major transition in the racial or ethnic composition of the membership, movement to a significantly different size, or the journey from a "chaplaincy" stance to a missional posture. We have also found that the most effective transformational leaders have mastered the *art* of leadership. They know when a congregation is ready to move forward and when it is time to slow down, regardless of any timetables that may have been previously set.

Congregational transformation has many analogies to whitewater rafting. Whitewater rafting is an exhilarating adventure, but it can also be dangerous if it is not done properly. Simply having experience with other watercraft—sailboats, rowboats, fishing boats—is insufficient. Before beginning, the right equipment must be gathered. The right kind of raft, oars, and life jackets are imperative. A wise rafting guide will include a first-aid kit, an emergency throw line, water and snacks for the journey, and other supplies. In the same way, spiritual and relational vitality must be in place to begin the transformation. Starting without this foundation is like heading down a raging river in a twelve-foot aluminum fishing boat.

For challenging raft trips, a map of the river is invaluable. Being warned of the approaching rapids or the need to portage around a waterfall is more than a "nice to know" luxury. A good river map recommends a particular approach to the tricky currents, highlights boulders hidden in the stream, and suggests places to stop for a rest or for scouting a difficult passage. But even the best map is limited in the amount of information that it can convey. Changes in the river's flow rate, weather conditions, or the abilities of the rafters may necessitate different approaches to the river. Obstacles that can be avoided easily at low flows may become major concerns when the river is running fast. So it is with the eight-stage change process. It provides many suggestions and insights for the change process, but actual conditions will always require real-time adjustments in the approach for a given congregation.

A specific set of skills is also needed for a successful whitewater journey. Anyone who decides to pilot the raft based exclusively on experience with other types of watercraft has made a serious mistake. Handling a raft bears no more resemblance to boating on a lake than riding a bike down the street does to driving an eighteen-wheeler on an interstate highway. Reading the currents, recognizing patterns in the water that point to hidden rocks, steering a clumsy rubber craft, timing the turns and paddle strokes are all essential skills for the whitewater environment. The learning disciplines facilitate transformation, just as rafting skills provide for safe passage on the river. And like the boater who has never been in whitewater, many church leaders underestimate the gap between their level of preparedness and the requirements for change leadership.

One of the great challenges of congregational transformation is that all three components must be done well and simultaneously. A transformational effort based on spiritual vitality without the change process or the learning disciplines is no more sensible than having the raft without the river map or the whitewater experience. All three are essential to successful transformations.

The interdependent nature of the three components is a challenge to many leaders. We acknowledge, without apology, that mastering and monitoring all three components simultaneously is not easy. We also assert that human beings are designed to master complex tasks. Those who make the commitment and stay the course will find great reward in the journey. It is our hope that this book provides encouragement and practical guidance that has emerged from our collective journey. It is ultimately our hope to contribute in some small way to the renewal of the church as we face some of its most challenging days.

Chapter 2

Spiritual and Relational Vitality

The Driving Force in Congregational Change

READ THE EARLY chapters of the book of Acts and it is clear that the church had a dynamic sense of power that is missing from many congregations today. "Everyone was filled with awe, and many wonders and miraculous signs were done by the apostles. . . . And the Lord was adding to their number daily those who were being saved" (Acts 2:43, 47b). The vitality that was present created a sense of awe that swept across the believers, and its impact on their lives was visible and powerful.

In the Congregational Transformation Model, spiritual and relational vitality is the core of the process. Without this vitality, the church becomes like any other organization or group of people. With it, the kind of transformation we advocate is not only possible, but likely.

Spiritual and relational vitality is the life-giving power that faithful people experience together as they passionately pursue God's vision for their lives. Individuals and congregations long to experience this kind of power. Unfortunately, many have given up hope of living with this vitality. The resistance to change and the cynicism we see may often be the consequences of people's past disappointments with the institutional church.

Spiritual and relational vitality are two dimensions of a single reality—a consistent teaching of Scripture. Jesus summed it up in this way. "One of them, an expert in the law, tested him with this question: 'Teacher, which is the greatest commandment in the Law?' Jesus replied: 'Love the Lord your God with all your heart and with all your soul and with all your mind. This is the first and greatest commandment. And the second is like it: Love your neighbor as yourself. All the Law and the Prophets hang on these two commandments'" (Matthew 22:35–40).

All of the law and the prophets are summarized by a commandment to love God (spiritual vitality) and to love our neighbor (relational vitality)—like two sides to the same coin. Unconditional love for our neighbors—with all of their idiosyncrasies and brokenness—is impossible unless we have a deep sense of the presence and power of God in our lives. The strongest indicator that our love for God is pure and obedient is when it results in a more faithful and effective expression of love for others. When we are out of balance, it diminishes our vitality and our capacity to influence our world.

If this is God's desire for his church—that it experiences life-giving power—how can it be achieved? This chapter seeks to address that question. The church described in Acts 2 had a unity of heart, mind, and spirit—and God added daily to their number! We all wish to be a part of a congregation for which this description is true. How is it possible for the church today to experience the transforming power that was experienced by the early church?

A Search for Vitality

Nearly two decades ago, Joe Aldrich, President of Multnomah Seminary, joined a group of pastors in the Portland (Oregon) area in seeking to answer the question "What does it take to attract and sustain the blessing of God on a geographic region?" They found themselves in an enormous mission field with churches struggling to make an impact. Church leaders felt a pervasive sense of discouragement. After studying the Scripture and seeking the heart of God together for several years, they came to understand and describe a process that seems to be operative every time the sustained blessing of God comes. Our framework for spiritual and relational vitality grows out of the work of Aldrich (1994) and the Multnomah team.

Clearly, God is greater than our understanding of him. We cannot box him into a process or a formula. According to Isaiah 55:8, God's ways are not our ways and his thoughts are not our thoughts. There is nothing that human beings can do to manipulate or force God into giving his blessing. On the other hand, God's ways are not hidden. He invites us to participate in his kingdom. From the very beginning of the human story he has been revealing himself to his people (Amos 4:13), calling them to live in covenant with him (Genesis 17:7 ff.), and empowering them to serve as a nation of priests to the world he seeks to redeem (1 Peter 2:9).

In order to live in this covenant relationship, there are things that only God can do and there are things that we must do. This chapter focuses on the latter. How can an individual believer or group of believers best posture themselves to experience and express the presence and power of God in their lives and congregations?

The fourfold process described in Figure 2.1 is built on the fundamental assumption that God's people must live as an authentic New Testament community like the one described in Acts 2:42–47. In the absence of a unified, authentic community, the church cannot become the salt and light it is called to be. Jesus prayed, "May they be brought to complete unity to let the world know that you sent me and have loved them even as you have loved me" (John 17:23). Spiritual and relational vitality is profoundly personal and corporate. It pervades all of our attitudes and our actions. It must be simultaneously routine and revolutionary.

Our description in this chapter follows the movement (clockwise) from an individual's encounter with God to the experience of grace, unity, and community. However, as the arrows on Figure 2.1 denote, the flow of influence moves both ways at the same time. God's presence in the gathered community leads to a spirit of shared unity, saving grace, and hunger for God.

How can we use this process to better understand and achieve spiritual and relational vitality? Clearly, we must have an ongoing *encounter* with *God's holiness*. The beginning of Isaiah 6 describes one such encounter. The worshiper came into the presence of God and encountered him in his beauty, power, and majesty. Out of this encounter, the worshiper *experienced God's grace* (Isaiah 6:5–7). He had a new perspective

FIGURE 2.1   Elements of Spiritual and Relational Vitality

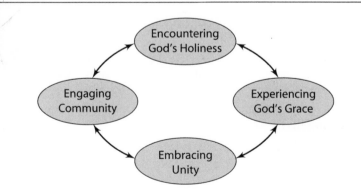

on his own broken and sinful nature, and he was moved to express deep humility. Ultimately he experienced that gift of grace in the forgiveness of his sin. This undeserved gift produced an overwhelming sense of gratitude. The same grace is available to everyone. The Gospel of John reminds us, "If we confess our sins, he is faithful and just and will forgive us our sins and purify us from all unrighteousness" (1 John 1:9).

The awareness of God's surpassing love changes our hearts. We recognize that every other person is a sinner who is offered this same gift of God's love. When we see others as equals, we are more willing to *embrace the spirit of unity.* The apostle Paul clearly states, "Make every effort to keep the unity of the Spirit through the bond of peace" (Ephesians 4:3). He also reminds us to consider others better than ourselves (Philippians 2:3).

Unity is important, but it does not represent the fullness of God's plan. His desire is that we *practice authentic Christian community.* The story of the New Testament church is one of believers being unified through the grace of God and changing their world as they lived in community with one another. God has equipped us to live in this community by giving individual believers different gifts and responsibilities. Ephesians 4 describes that God gives each of us a different role in the church, but the common purpose is "that the body of Christ may be built up until we all reach unity in the faith and in the knowledge of the Son of God and become mature, attaining to the whole measure of the fullness of Christ" (Ephesians 4:12–13).

Unity and community are not to be confused with uniformity. The passage in Ephesians and the analogies of the church as a body (Romans 12, 1 Corinthians 12, Colossians 3) clearly affirm the importance of diversity within the church. Nor is the call to keep unity a command to squelch conflict. When a group of individuals are committed to a common purpose, their diversity will often lead to disagreement. In the New Testament, conflict is often present. There are times when it is life-giving (see Acts 6:1–7 and Acts 11:1–18) and times when it is life-threatening (see 1 and 2 Corinthians). Living in community is a challenge, but it is also a powerful experience that can bring us back to an encounter with the holiness of God.

Encountering God's Holiness!

Effective change leaders consistently serve as catalysts to help people encounter the holiness of God. The fundamental calling of the Christian faith is to worship God. The call of discipleship is to radically reorder life's decisions around the one true living God and his claim to our lives. To respond to this call faithfully and effectively, we must experience life-changing encounters with God in the body of Christ as a regular discipline.

While God initiates reconciliation with us, what can we do as disciples and as leaders to respond appropriately? Our general framework is centered around personal and corporate worship. The specific ways in which worship is expressed will be unique to each person and congregation.

Individually the change leader must consistently encounter the holiness of God. In countless conversations, pastors acknowledge that a regular time to be still and quiet in the presence of God is often the first thing to be dropped from their pressing schedules. Reading Scripture, praying, experiencing prolonged periods of solitude, fasting, studying, resting, and relaxing in nature are all means that increase our likelihood of encountering the presence of God. Richard Foster's classic book *Celebration of Discipline* (1988) is a clarion call to the historic Christian disciplines that refresh and empower the people of God. *Experiencing God*, by Henry Blackaby and Claude King (1990), has helped many Christians and congregations establish or rekindle a deep, personal, ongoing encounter with God.

Spiritual and relational vitality also means encountering the holiness of God corporately. The church expresses this most clearly in corporate worship. A church cannot be on mission with God without an energizing corporate worship experience that helps the body encounter God's holiness.

Beyond "Sunday morning" corporate worship, congregations need to clearly encounter God as they make plans to achieve his vision. Blackaby and King call the church to identify the activity of God and join him in that activity (1990, pp. 64–71). Far too often, congregations assume that they are prepared to deal with the things of God. This can result in making plans and asking God to bless them. A planning process may focus on controlling our future rather than aligning our lives with God's activity. When worship is at the heart of planning, we are more likely to focus on aligning all of our lives—individually and corporately—with the ongoing activity of God among us.

In helping congregations focus on spiritual and relational vitality as a key component of transformation process, worship is integral to the process. We might start a meeting by saying, "Just because we are the people of God, let's not automatically assume that we are prepared to discern and engage in the things of God. Let's spend some time in worship first.

Let's do everything we can to be in a position to know the direction of God." We then spend fifteen to thirty minutes in an intentional worship experience, confessing our sin, acknowledging our fears, and offering ourselves to God's service.

Taking time for worship makes the planning process much less efficient, but it also makes it much more effective. Encountering the holiness of God is not something that is limited to our personal or corporate worship gatherings. It must become a way of life that transforms our personal hearts and minds (Romans 12:1–2).

Trinity Church was once a large, growing church making a significant impact in its community. But those days were long gone. For more than thirty-five years the congregation had experienced declines in attendance and morale. Its efforts to regain a sense of spiritual and relational vitality had been futile. In 1992, thirty-five-year-old Emerson Gonzales was called to be the new pastor.

In the early days of his work, Emerson called the congregation to look to the future. He assured them that their best days were ahead, but experiencing that future would require a willingness to give up everything and return to a passionate love for Christ. In one of his first sermons he said, "If we will seek Jesus and him alone, the concerns we have and the challenges we face will come into perspective."

Over the next two years Emerson focused on the goal of helping the congregation renew its spiritual and relational vitality. One key event was a two-day retreat for the elected and informal leaders of the congregation. The sole purpose of the retreat was to create the space and focus that would allow the leaders to encounter God. Emerson resisted the temptation to fill the agenda with planning for the future. The entire weekend was spent worshiping together and alone, studying Scripture, and praying. Some of the leaders fasted throughout the retreat.

At the conclusion of the retreat, Emerson asked people to express what they had experienced. Some expressed a sense of hope. Others expressed their despair over the long decline of the church. Some confessed sins of bitterness and lack of faith.

As the retreat came to an end, the Pastor said: "I know some of you expect me to have come with a program or an agenda to turn the church around. I want to tell you as clearly as I can that the only agenda I have for now is to repeatedly call us back into the presence of God. Don't misinterpret what I'm saying—I firmly believe God has a plan for us. But I want us to be sure that the plan we commit to is God's, not ours. I don't know when or how he will reveal that plan. Until he makes it clear, I want to ask you as leaders in Trinity Church to join me in calling the rest of this body of Christ back to its first love."

This retreat was the beginning of a turnaround at Trinity. In the weeks that followed, several individuals reported incidents of reconciliation over past conflict and renewed commitment to following God. But the process was not painless. Emerson and several key leaders were also criticized for not taking more initiative to "fix" the challenges that the church faced. Ultimately their persistence paid off by providing the power needed for major changes in direction.

Experiencing God's Grace!

Encountering the holiness of God always has the effect of creating humility. We cannot help but see the stark contrast between ourselves and God's majesty, power, and love. In this experience, we affirm our brokenness and we remember at the deepest level that we are the creatures and God is the creator. When we experience God's gift of grace—forgiveness—our hearts are changed. If our hearts are hardened and we do not experience humility and grace, spiritual and relational vitality is not possible.

Effective change leaders help others make the connection between individual experiences of grace and the need to extend that grace to all of life's relationships. They seek to foster a spirit of grace throughout the network of relationships in the congregation. They begin by assessing their own network of relationships for any unresolved conflict. Have they alienated or offended others? Credibility is significantly strengthened when the change leader takes action to humbly seek forgiveness and reconciliation.

Effective change leaders will probably be aware of relationships in the larger congregation that are not what they should be. By gently nurturing individuals to extend grace and forgiveness to one another, the change leaders serve as catalysts for reconciliation. The congregation's heritage may hold glaring experiences that need reconciliation. Pastors have a powerful opportunity to preach God's grace and to tell stories that will encourage and inspire others to live in humility and grace.

In Trinity Church, this grace became increasingly evident. One of the leaders who had attended the retreat felt compelled to begin a weekly men's prayer group. The group grew to twenty regular participants. As individual men began openly to share the tough challenges in their lives, grace and accountability were experienced and expressed. Memorizing

Scripture became a regular discipline of the group. Real life change began to emerge.

Several other groups emerged spontaneously over the next year. One longtime member observed, "I can't remember a time when more people were praying more often in this church." The results could be seen in many aspects of the congregation's life. Worship seemed to take on an added intensity. Morale was increasingly positive. Conflict that occurred was managed in a more redemptive fashion. Slowly, imperceptibly at first, corporate worship attendance began increasing.

It was during this time that Robert Young, a longtime member and deacon at Trinity, came to see Pastor Gonzales. As the conversation unfolded, Robert said, "Pastor, in my personal time with God, I keep remembering an experience that we had here about fourteen years ago. We told you about it when you interviewed for the job, but I've become convinced that it is a more important incident than we have acknowledged."

A former pastor of the church had confessed to the deacons that he was involved in an adulterous relationship with one of the church's members. The deacons had no experience dealing with such a situation. Together they decided that the pastor should resign. The next Sunday the deacons made the announcement that he had resigned and would not return, but gave no further explanation. The fallout from the incident was severe. Rumors were rampant. Some people accused the deacons of running the pastor off. In the end, the real story leaked out, but the congregation's sense of trust had been violated and twenty families had left the church.

Robert Young concluded his story by saying: "I keep having the sense that until we go back and attempt to redeem that situation, we are always going to be hamstrung in our efforts to have an impact on the community. What should we do?"

They agreed to discuss the matter with the current deacons. At first there was resistance among the deacons to dealing with this old issue. "Why should we drag that skeleton out of the closet?" After several weeks of conversation and prayer, however, they agreed that Emerson and Robert should seek out the former pastor and see how God might bring healing to this relationship.

When they eventually located him, they were surprised that he was eager to meet. The ensuing meeting was emotional. The pastor had left the ministry and had lived in deep remorse for years over the consequences of his actions on the church and both families. His alienation from the church only made the suffering worse. He had longed to confess and to ask forgiveness but saw no opportunity of finding a listening ear at his former church.

Emerson and Robert extended forgiveness to this former pastor and asked for his forgiveness as well. They confessed that the church had not followed the teaching of Scripture and sought to be redemptive with him. The former pastor extended forgiveness as well.

Emerson and Robert reported this experience to the deacons, and agreed that no further action needed to be taken. They had a firm sense that a difficult chapter in the congregation's history had finally been closed. Even though no scientific connection can be made, Emerson Gonzales looks back to this experience of reconciliation as a key turning point in the congregation's life.

Embracing Our Unity!

The experience of grace and humility is an empowering one. We live in the awareness that we must trust and follow God. We are freed from the need to live with the pretense of being in control. That pretense separates us from one another. It causes us to grasp for power and protect our fragile egos. It compels us to jockey for position so that we can protect our vested interests.

When we encounter God and see ourselves for who we are, we are free to embrace one another. If the perfect and almighty God can forgive us, how can we not forgive others? How can we hold a grudge or not give a fellow church member the benefit of the doubt? We all stand equal at the foot of the cross. There is a powerful, euphoric feeling that comes with that recognition. There is solidarity and a fellowship that is life giving. As we come to understand God's purposes, our devotion to him calls us to unity with others who have experienced his grace.

Effective change leaders continually hold up the mission or purpose of the church as the basis for unity. They call people to commitment by describing and pursuing the biblical mission of the church. That mission becomes a foundation that allows the Holy Spirit to work in the hearts of people.

Congregational leaders must recognize the tension between unity and diversity and affirm both as essential in God's plan. They find examples of these two dynamics simultaneously at work and highlight them for the congregation. If this continuum is out of balance on one end, it creates a sense of conformity and superficial unity. If it is out of balance on the other end, tolerance is expressed instead of unity. Focusing on God's mission will challenge the congregation to fully employ its diversity and its creative energies.

Individual testimonies are another effective way to foster unity. New members who feel a deep sense of connection can tell why they chose to become a part of the congregation. Longtime members can reflect on past and present experiences that call them to commitment for the future.

Two years after the reconciliation with Trinity's former pastor, Emerson reflected: "It seemed that the spiritual and relational vitality of our church took a dramatic turn after that experience. Worship services seemed more alive. I heard other individual stories of reconciliation. The fellowship following worship services seemed more vibrant. It was just a different place."

Emerson and other leaders in the congregation had also begun sensing greater urgency to clarify the specific vision God had for Trinity Church. In his Sunday morning sermon a few weeks later, he addressed this challenge.

We have experienced God's healing in some important ways over the last three years, and God has strengthened us as a church family. I have heard a number of you saying that the congregation seems more unified than it has been in a long time. I want to remind you that unity is a fragile experience. It is something that we must constantly nurture. Many forces at work around us and within us will challenge that unity. As Paul said in Ephesians 6:12, "For our struggle is not against flesh and blood, but against the rulers, against the authorities, against the powers of this dark world and against the spiritual forces of evil in the heavenly realms."

Jesus prayed in John 17 that his followers would be unified. It's time for us to take the next steps in our congregational life. We must seek the Lord's leadership as we clarify his vision for this congregation. In our unity he will speak. But in the process, our unity will be challenged.

I want us to begin praying very specifically about how we will discern God's vision for our congregation. The easiest thing in the world to do is to rush out and put our plans together. But we want to know God's plan for us.

Engaging Community!

Unity must be translated into community if God's people are to have an ongoing impact in the world. Unity is found in God's mission.

Community is experienced as sinful, broken, and highly diverse people joyfully pursue this mission in ways that reflect the character and spirit of Jesus. Paul describes Christian community as the body of Christ. "The body is a unit, though it is made up of many parts; and though all its parts are many, they form one body. So it is with Christ" (1 Corinthians 12:12). As we join together in the body, we are able to serve him more effectively.

Effective change leaders intentionally foster experiences that allow disciples to mature and develop. For the congregation to have the spiritual and relational vitality needed to transform the world around them, more of its members must act more like Jesus.

Living together in community is always challenging. Effective change leaders develop conflict management skills and help others in the congregation do the same. They are proactive about listening and discerning potential rifts in the fabric of community life. The issues underlying these rifts should be proactively addressed. If they are allowed to fester, they can become real threats to the community life.

Martha Tomlinson was a sixty-year-old leader who had been a member of Trinity for fourteen years. Pastor Emerson asked her to give a testimony describing values that Jesus taught that seemed most evident at Trinity Church. Martha did her usual thorough job in her assignment. She talked about revelation, people, and stability as values that had guided Trinity Church for the past fourteen years.

When the worship service was over, John Clarion stopped Martha in the parking lot. John was thirty-one and was the youngest and shortest-tenured member of the Pastor Advisory Team.

"I appreciated what you said today. You are a very effective communicator. Thanks for sharing with us. I've just got one question for you. How do we value stability if the church's mission is about change?"

Martha answered, "Well, I don't know that I believe the church's mission is about change. Our church has been pursuing God's mission for a long time and we've not had a lot of change."

John replied, "I like many things about our church. In the time I've been here, God has blessed me in many ways. But there are some things that are going to have to change if we are going to do everything I believe God wants us to do."

"Like what?" Martha asked.

"Well, like our worship services."

Martha tensed. She had participated in several conversations over the past few months in which she learned that the younger members of the church wanted to change the format and musical style of the worship service. "What's wrong with our worship services?"

"It's not that there is anything wrong. It's just that I think they could be improved. Doing so will help us reach more people in the community who are my age," was his reply.

About that time Emerson walked up and joined in the conversation. He took advantage of the opportunity to lift the level of the conversation. He challenged Martha and John to focus on discerning what God wanted rather than on their personal preferences. He acknowledged that both had strong and valid opinions, and he stressed the importance of unity and diversity within the body.

"If we will keep focusing on our relationship with God and his purposes for the church, we will be going in the right direction. I believe he will help us come to some consensus around the values that will guide the process—biblical values that will undergird our decision making. Then we'll be more likely to face individual choices—and individual differences—well.

"I know this is not going to be easy. That's why we are taking it slow. It's also why at every step along the way we've got to seek the Lord. We've got to commit to each other and to him to discern his direction. This is not about what we want."

Despite the obvious tension, Emerson was pleased with the conversation. It reflected the challenge of change and of staying focused on purpose in the midst of diversity. It was one of hundreds that he had as the congregation's life unfolded. He reflected, "Proactively guarding the integrity of the community is a never-ending process."

The Importance of the Process

In our experience, individual change leaders and congregations often short-circuit the process of allowing the Holy Spirit to foster a strong sense of spiritual and relational vitality. In a world that demands instant results, we want a process in which everything happens quickly. We pray a cursory prayer at the beginning of a meeting, we engage the process with all of the baggage of our brokenness, and we ask God to bless us once we have decided what we want to do.

The resounding message of this book is that without authentic spiritual and relational vitality in a local gathering of believers, the church does not have the resources that are demanded to engage transformation and to influence the world. As the pace of change accelerates, the demand for this power is only going to increase.

Chapter 3

Laying the Groundwork for Change

GLENWOOD COMMUNITY CHURCH was formed in 1986 in a growing new suburban community. The church grew rapidly, primarily by the addition of "churched" people who moved into the area. Within three years, average attendance had grown to 225. But by 1991, Pastor Russ Osterman began to realize that change was necessary. The church was being recognized by its denomination for its growth, but Russ knew that they were not truly achieving their mission of reaching unchurched people. "It was a very confusing time. I took the lack of baptisms very personally. I told myself that I was an ineffective preacher and that the failure was mine." During a vacation with his wife, the Lord made it clear to Osterman that he was not to leave. In his prayer, he asked God, "Show me a church that is reaching unchurched people."

Soon after his return from vacation, he had an opportunity to attend a seminar at Saddleback Community Church in California. Seeing and experiencing the model of a dynamic congregation that was truly reaching unchurched people had a deep impact on Russ, and he returned to Glenwood a changed person. He had no experience in change leadership and no road map for how to lead congregational transformation, but he had a heart for unchurched people. Russ began to lead his church to embrace a new model based on what he had learned.

To his surprise, many in the congregation responded with anger and frustration. "I did not have any training in processing change in the church. I probably only survived because I'm such an aggressive leader who could endure the conflict." By the end of 1991, attendance had dropped to eighty people and the church was $30,000 in arrears.

The Glenwood story illustrates the perilous experience of many change leaders. Those who have a clear sense of God's mission, and an equally acute sense of despair or frustration over the state of their church, may feel a strong urge to ask, "Do I have to spend so much time on groundwork?" Or at the very least, "How quickly can I get through these stages so that we can start doing the *real* work that will have a meaningful impact?"

This chapter describes the first three stages of the change process. These early stages of the change process will be a difficult period for leaders motivated by tangible and public results. They will constantly fight self-imposed, and sometimes externally imposed, pressures to move ahead with the process. These early stages are, by definition, not highly visible.

In our experience, laying the groundwork properly in the first three stages is critical to the ultimate success of the change process. It is possible to jump straight to vision development and then announce the new vision to the congregation. But when implementation of the vision begins, the likelihood of controversy, resistance, or apathy will increase significantly. Either the congregation will not understand why certain actions are necessary, or they will refuse to support them. These steps are just as important for starting a new congregation or for "young" churches that are dealing with a major change for the first time. The only exception is when the whole congregation agrees that a crisis is at hand, and the members are willing to trust the key leaders to make decisions. In this instance, it may be necessary to take immediate actions that represent a dramatic shift in the congregation's direction.

The early stages of the change process enable the pastor and other leaders in the congregation to demonstrate why change is needed and to build the support that leads to a state of *change-readiness*. Stages 1 to 3—making personal preparation, creating urgency, and establishing the vision community—take the church to the point of being prepared to change and of needing clear direction for its transformation.

Stage 1: Making Personal Preparation

No one begins a major building program with hammer and nails. Construction projects require careful planning and preparation in order to make the best use of resources. This means analyzing the needs and proposed uses, considering financial capabilities, discussing the possibilities with the congregation, and obtaining outside expertise. It is much more expensive to make a change after construction has started than during the design stage. In the same way, the change process begins long before God's vision is discerned, a key program is redesigned, or the organization is restructured.

Preparation is essential, but the temptation to skip this stage is powerful. Pastor and congregational leaders face enormous stress. There are always too many things to do and too many fires to fight. Unfortunately, one frequent result of these pressures is their failure to invest in the things that can have the greatest long-term impact on their congregations. If leaders cannot or will not make the time to prepare adequately for transformation, they should not continue any further with the process.

Taking the time for adequate preparation is a clear biblical principle. Moses spent considerable time in the desert before leading the people out of Egypt. Nehemiah heard the report from his countrymen, and entered into a period of intense prayer before confronting the king. Jesus spent far more time in preparation than he did in his recorded public ministry. God uses times of preparation to communicate with his servants and to prepare them for the great tasks that lie ahead.

We have already discussed the core dimension of spiritual and relational vitality. It serves to create an underlying state of readiness for the leaders and the congregation to experience God's desired transformation: "Here I am Lord, send me." Once the leaders sense a readiness for change, the time of personal preparation focuses on the specific ways in which God is leading: "Exactly what do you want me to be *willing* to do about this situation, Lord?"

The time of personal preparation allows the pastor and other key leaders to get ready for the journey that lies ahead. Making personal preparation means becoming increasingly open to hearing God's voice and to making the personal and congregational changes that may be required. It means dealing with personal issues and motivations that might get in the way of the transformation. It means taking the time to rest and recharge—both physically and mentally—before embarking on a long journey. Personal preparation has everything to do with the journey of seeing and following God's vision.

Suggested Actions to Foster Change

For each stage in the change process, we offer suggested actions to be taken. These are not the only possible ways of moving the church through the stages of change. Our expectation is that the change leaders in the congregation will start by examining and understanding the objectives of a particular stage. They will then develop their own unique approach, which may include some of the suggested actions, some modified actions, and some entirely different steps for accomplishing the goals. Readers will also find a certain amount of overlap between the actions in different parts of the model. Continuous interaction between various parts is one of the central characteristics of transformation.

Practice Spiritual Disciplines

Personal preparation must begin with the consistent practice of the spiritual disciplines. Transformation is a process of bringing the church into alignment with God's unique vision. If the leaders of the congregation are not spending significant, consistent time seeking God's direction—through prayer, Bible study, meditation, solitude, and fasting—it will be impossible for meaningful and lasting transformation to occur. In addition to a daily time with God, personal retreats can be a very effective way to prepare and recharge.

Revisit God's Mission for the Church

Through regular times with God, the leader should begin to gain a renewed sense of God's mission for the church. Study of some of the powerful Bible passages relating to the Lord's guidance—Nehemiah, the Exodus from Egypt, Paul's missionary journey—can be especially helpful. Even though vision development as a formal step is not addressed until later in the process, change leaders need a renewed sense of how God can and does work in the world and of his call to all Christians.

The simple process of intentionally stepping away from the daily grind, of focusing on the future, and of being inspired by powerful stories of God leading his people can change a leader's perspective. In the "busy-ness" of life, we quickly shift to the tactical thinking of weekly plans and set our sights on incremental improvement. God has a much bigger plan, and our task is to create openness in our lives where we can begin to see this. As elements of God's plans become clear, the leader should make notes for future reference.

Conduct an Honest Self-Assessment

The leaders of effective transformations are honest with God and with themselves. They understand that the best way to lead their congregations, particularly through challenging times, is to have a realistic understanding of their own capabilities and shortcomings. Therefore, they spend time looking at their motives, fears, gifts, and faults. This self-assessment should clarify how they tend to lead, where they will need help, and what pitfalls they should seek to avoid. One leader may recognize that he does not listen well in a group setting when his opinion is challenged. He may ask a few trusted peers to "help him listen." Another leader may become aware that her fear of conflict and disapproval prevents her from making critical decisions. In this self-assessment, leaders may also recognize a need to experience specific healing through confession and forgiveness around a particular issue.

Be Accountable

In addition to self-assessment, transformational leaders need to have a sense of outside accountability. Just as God used Nathan to confront David about his adulterous relationship with Bathsheba (2 Samuel 12), fellow Christians are an important tool that God uses to encourage, challenge, and rebuke today's leaders. We all have blind spots that prevent us from accurately evaluating ourselves. One leader may consider interpersonal skills to be a forte and not recognize a trail of damaged relationships in his wake. Another may view herself as an outstanding communicator and then blame it on the listeners when they fail to understand. Regardless of our individual flaws, we can all improve our effectiveness with wise counsel from other trusted Christians.

This help can come from an accountability group, a peer in ministry, or a trusted mentor. An accountable leader is willing to acknowledge fears and failings to these trusted friends. They may find that the leader has been too critical in his self-assessment, or that she has overlooked an important issue. Over time, they can challenge and encourage the leader. The pastor who struggles with humility when the church is growing may need to be reminded that it is God's church. The controlling leader who hesitates to delegate important tasks may need to be encouraged that her development of other leaders is just as important as "doing the job right." The undisciplined minister who consistently fails to complete tasks on time may become more proficient simply from knowing that his peers are going to ask whether he is on schedule.

Proactively Address Problems

Self-assessment and accountability will often reveal specific issues that need to be resolved at an individual, ministry, or congregational level. If the issue is serious enough, it will affect the church's spiritual and relational vitality and may require that the change process be slowed down while resolution is sought. A damaged relationship may need to be repaired. A congregational decision may have been "railroaded." A group within the church may have been made to feel unimportant after being excluded from an important decision. The time of personal preparation is the best time to seek healing for these concerns. Failure to do so loads the change process down with unnecessary baggage.

Unresolved problems, whether large or small, whether the pastor is directly involved or not, can undermine transformation. A humble and honest "I'm sorry" can begin to bring healing in the life of an angry or apathetic member. When relationships are not what God intends, it is more difficult for the church to experience authentic unity around God's vision.

Find the Right Pace
Finally, the time of personal preparation is a time for the pastor to develop a sense of pace for the process that lies ahead. Some change leaders will have a tendency to rush ahead because of their intense desire to accomplish something. For others, the fear of conflict or of the unknown pushes them to procrastinate endlessly. By recognizing personal tendencies, by seeking God's direction, and by being open to the input of trusted advisors, change leaders can begin to find the right pace.

The Benefits of Making Personal Preparation
Personal preparation is an essential first step for the change process. It is closely related to the core element of spiritual and relational vitality and to the discipline of personal mastery. The specific benefits of this stage are

- Focusing on relationship with God from the start of the process, and relying on his wisdom and guidance
- Developing a spirit of openness to whatever deep personal changes may be required
- Establishing firmly the spiritual disciplines that are needed to carry the leader throughout the remainder of the process
- Planting the seeds from which a clear vision will grow
- Increasing sensitivity to the concerns of other people
- Dealing with potential obstacles in a positive and proactive manner

Key Challenge in Making Personal Preparation

*Carving out the time and space to discern God's voice and
direction for the leader's own ministry and for the church,
and living with the tension that this creates.*

When is the right time to move beyond the personal preparation stage? We do not offer formulas for the length of time needed in this or any other stage. The transformation process cannot have a rigid timeline. We encourage leaders to be patient and to evaluate whether they have prepared adequately before moving to the next stage. This same attitude of patience and ongoing assessment is important throughout the change process. In the workbook, we offer several specific questions to assist leaders with their evaluation for each of the eight stages.

In his letter to the church in Corinth, the apostle Paul says, "Run in such a way as to get the prize. Everyone who competes in the games goes into strict training. They do it to get a crown that will not last; but we do it to get a crown that will last forever" (1 Corinthians 9:24–25). Paul clearly understood the importance of preparation.

Stage 2: Creating Urgency

"Do we have to go through this stage in the change process?" Just the word *urgency* elicits strong reactions, and in many cases the associated images are negative. The short answer is that urgency is absolutely necessary in congregational transformation. When used properly, urgency is a positive driver for change. *Creating urgency*, as described in this model, refers to the energy and motivation for change that is generated by contrasting between an accurate perception of reality and God's ideal. (See Chapter Seven for additional information regarding creating urgency.)

If a doctor told you that he would like to begin a round of chemotherapy, based on a single incident of cancer in your extended family, you would find another doctor. No matter how highly recommended or well qualified he was, you would seriously question this anecdotal and seemingly unsupported diagnosis. However, if you had noticed changes in your health and had received confirmation of a tumor through the most accurate medical procedures, you would be much more willing to accept the need for treatment, no matter how undesirable the side effects might be. The urgency would be the result of your clear perception of the situation and your image of a healthy, cancer-free body. Creating urgency is an essential diagnostic step that must precede the ultimate "treatment" of the change process.

Many evangelical Christian leaders in the United States feel a growing sense of urgency. George Barna, a popular observer of the church and its interaction with our society writes, "At this moment of optimum opportunity, Christianity is having less impact on people's perspectives and behaviors than ever. Why is that? Because a growing majority of people have dismissed the Christian faith as weak, outdated, and irrelevant" (1998, p. 5).

Urgency is critical in the individual congregation. It creates a driving force that makes the organization willing to accept change and to challenge the conventional wisdom. It is no wonder that so many churches seem unwilling to change—they lack any sense of urgency. Congregations often avoid quantification ("the movement of God's Spirit can't be measured"), rationalize away warning signals ("attendance was poor, but there was a very good spirit among those who were present"), sugarcoat bad news, and avoid anything that could seem like individual blame. Successful businesses have learned that they need a continuous flow of outside information in order to survive. Christian churches should not be run like secular businesses, but they should not use this as an excuse to avoid the truth.

At the other end of the continuum are the churches that treat everything as a crisis. Whether it is an unending diet of "the end of the world" from the pulpit or a "crisis of the week" culture, the congregation becomes immune to the underlying issues that should cause a real sense of urgency. Just like the boy who cried wolf, these congregations become capable of ignoring the message even when pressing issues are raised.

A congregation does not need to have a vision statement to understand God's ideal. This ideal, which we refer to as *mission* may reflect powerful biblical mandates like the Great Commission (Matthew 28:19–20), the Great Commandment (Matthew 22:37–40), other key passages (such as Luke 4:17–19), or one of the powerful creeds of the early church (Apostles', Nicene). Regardless of the specific passages that we might use, the New Testament principles of worshiping God, loving other human beings, and making disciples are unarguable mandates. This is best reflected in the life of the early church as depicted in Acts. *Mission,* as we define the term, is not unique to a particular church—it is similar for all Christian congregations. For a congregation that is characterized by apathy or decline, engaging these teachings with renewed vigor and looking thoughtfully at its own situation should begin to create urgency.

Creating urgency does not necessarily portray the church in a negative light. Some of the most urgent churches in the country are those that are vitally concerned about the people in their communities who are dying without the knowledge of God's love. Urgency can be created by a strong awareness of the unchurched mission field that is outside the doors of nearly every church in America.

Urgency is found throughout the Old and New Testaments. The prophets repeatedly showed the people of Israel their true state and declared divine directives to emphasize how far they had strayed from God's plan. John the Baptist's message created a deep sense of urgency, so much that the people responded, "What should we do then?" (Luke 3:10), and even the tax collectors and soldiers were touched. Jesus' statement that "the harvest is plentiful but the workers are few" (Matthew 9:37) resonated deeply with an audience that lived off the land.

When urgency is fostered, it should lead the congregation to begin asking, just as people did upon hearing John the Baptist, "What are we going to do now?" This is a significant step. Implicit in this is the recognition that the status quo is not acceptable.

Urgency should lead to an increased openness to God and a greater willingness to change. But in many congregations today, the "urgency" that is expressed in the face of steady decline is not producing the desired results. Participants become concerned about whether the church will survive. Energy generated primarily by anxiety and fear is prone to nostalgic goals and self-protective strategies. Unhealthy urgency often becomes inwardly focused, rallying around a cry to preserve the institution rather than following God. Change leaders play a critical role in these situations by keeping the congregation focused on God and the future. Hope, vision, and a passion to be right with God and with others are the best tools to propel a healthy sense of urgency.

The creation of urgency typically has other consequences that many congregational leaders would prefer to avoid—conflict, denial, and resignation. Some members will be offended by a stark description of the gap between the church's current reality and God's ideal. Their paradigm of church is that problems and bad news are not discussed in a public forum. Others will resist in anticipation of the changes that are likely to follow. They know subconsciously that change is needed, but this means moving outside their comfort zones. Wise leaders understand that some resistance is inevitable, but they know that an accurate perception of reality is necessary for learning and growth. They recognize that instability in some people's personal lives causes them to over-react against any effort to stimulate discomfort. They also find ways to strike the right balance between too much discomfort and a watered down message that fails to build readiness for change.

In 1993, James Carson became pastor of Southside Baptist Church. The church was once a rural congregation ten miles outside the city. As the city grew outward, the church found itself swallowed by the city's booming suburbs, and made the transition from rural congregation to rapidly growing urban congregation. In 1958, it reached its apex in size when it completed a new worship center that seated twenty-two hundred. From 1958 to 1993, the community aged and transitioned, and the church declined. At first, the change in attendance was almost imperceptible. As the decline accelerated, conflict erupted, which created a vicious downward spiral. When Carson arrived, average attendance was only two hundred eighty.

On his first Sunday at Southside, Carson stood in the pulpit and said: "This congregation has been in decline for thirty-five years. We must face that reality squarely. If there is any possibility that God is going to use us to bring hope to this city, we must be very clear about our reality." Each member was given a graph of the attendance trends.

In looking back, Carson says, "That Sunday was the beginning of a turnaround. When we quit pretending and looked squarely in the face of reality, God created a sense of urgency in us." Five years later, Southside has grown to an average attendance of four hundred twenty. In 1997 it baptized sixty-eight people—more than the previous three years combined.

Suggested Actions to Foster Change

Creating urgency is like preparing a field for planting. The farmer knows that the harvest will not come until the autumn. His goal in the spring is to establish the right conditions for a bounteous future harvest. When done correctly, urgency establishes a powerful, early momentum to push the process in the right direction. Urgency can be created with a variety of specific steps.

Accurately Assess and Describe Current Reality

Businesses have a bottom line to watch, and business leaders are trained to measure nearly everything. Churches, on the other hand, tend to do little measurement and are often unsure what to do with the data they have. Information from trend analysis, congregational surveys, demographic studies, feedback, and interviews is relatively easy to obtain and can paint a much clearer picture of reality. Even when data are available, they are often not captured and presented in a manner that tells a compelling story.

This is not to say that hard quantitative facts are the only way to describe current reality. Just as some members respond to tables and graphs, others will respond to stories and images. The story of the visitor who could not find a class and left without being greeted paints a graphic image of the church's inward focus. The testimony of an incarcerated person's conversion through the church's prison ministry illustrates the potential to influence the community. A number of ideas for measuring and describing current reality are provided in the workbook that accompanies this text. An accurate description of the congregation's current state of affairs is a basic building block of this stage, and is critical for other stages as well.

Make Information Widely Available

Developing an accurate description of reality is critical, but it is of no value unless the information is readily available and clearly understood by the congregation. Congregational leaders often make two erroneous assumptions. They believe that everyone is already aware of the factual information. For example, they assume that changes in attendance patterns over a period of time are readily apparent to the membership. The average member may recollect that "it seemed that there were more people here last year," but she is hard pressed to see the overall trend. Leaders also assume that members will be able to arrive at the appropriate conclusions if they are presented with the raw data. "If we show them the downward trend in giving, they will understand the underlying causes and will realize what needs to be done to address them."

The way in which information is presented affects the sense of urgency. Change leaders take the time to tell the story from the data. The format and frequency of communications about the state of the church has a direct bearing on how the congregation perceives the problem. James Carson of Southside provides an instructive example of this. He used visual and verbal ways to communicate, and he continues to present information regularly on the state of the church today.

Seek Assistance

When presented well, the description of reality can be readily grasped. But performing this type of comprehensive and quantitative assessment is not a common skill. In most congregations there are individuals for whom analytical work is nearly second nature. They should be recruited to assist in the effort. The involvement of someone who can see what kinds of questions to ask, who can pick out trends and cause-effect relationships, and who can make a coherent presentation out of a mass of data will greatly contribute to the outcome of this stage.

Conduct a Congregational Assessment

A surprisingly large number of church leaders avoid feedback. They seem to have no interest in getting an accurate reading on the congregation's pulse. A comprehensive assessment tool can provide a broad indication of the perception of the membership. A survey highlights the areas of relative strength, or health, and the areas that currently need the most attention. If a majority of the members strongly disagree with the statement "Our worship services are inspirational," this should send a clear message to the leadership and should add specificity to the general sense of urgency. In addition to creating urgency, this type of tool is extremely useful in later stages of the change process. Periodic surveys can show important trends for consideration in the ongoing design of the change process.

Make Honesty and Constructive Criticism the Accepted and Expected Behavior

It will be difficult to create urgency if the church has a culture in which honest feedback is discouraged. No one wants to say that the reason the church fails to attract young families is that the children's Bible study uses out-of-date material and the leaders don't connect with the class. However, if this is a widely shared perception, it is essential that the leaders be able to discuss this. In other churches, the authority figures (pastor, other staff, key lay leaders) are never questioned, but an inability to discuss the honest perceptions of those in the congregation or the community cripples the change process.

Being honest does not mean displaying the brutal candor and adversarial attitudes that abound elsewhere in our society. The church is called to be a place of grace and acceptance for all. "Speak the truth in love"

(Ephesians 4:15). This is one of the greatest challenges in the early stages of the change process. If faithful volunteers perceive that their years of hard work are being criticized or even blamed for the church's current problems, irreparable damage can be done. They may leave or they may resist, but they are unlikely to be supportive of the needed changes.

The process of giving honest feedback needs to start with the key leaders. Pastors should be the ones to set this tone. They might talk or write about how the culture needs to become more open. They can make sure that longtime members feel appreciated. They can model the desired behavior by discussing the feedback from a survey (positive and negative) and how they personally plan to make adjustments. They can also invest extra time for dialogue concerning an important decision or call key members to solicit their opinions. When the senior leaders demonstrate openness, they earn the right to ask other leaders to do the same.

The Benefits of Creating Urgency

Urgency, as described here, is the fuel that launches the change process. When oxygen and hydrogen are stored separately, nothing happens. When they are carefully mixed together, the reaction creates an explosive force that can propel a space shuttle out of the earth's gravitational field. So it is with an accurate depiction of current reality and a growing understanding of God's ideal. Even though it is tempting to avoid this stage, the benefits are significant. They include

- Creating a clear picture of the church's current state that is widely shared by the congregation
- Providing a driving force for change and a willingness to accept new initiatives
- Making the status quo unacceptable
- Giving insight to the church's leadership about potential priorities for the change process

Key Challenge in Creating Urgency

*Creating energy for change: being clear and explicit
about current reality in contrast to God's ideal.*

Accurately describing reality and creating urgency makes people uncomfortable. It is designed to do so. Many in the church will directly or indirectly try to eliminate this tension as quickly as possible. They may disagree with the assessment ("You're not looking at the right data"), try to make relative comparisons ("I know that we've been declining, but we're doing a lot better than the church down the street"), or act the part of the "wounded saint" ("This information makes me feel so inadequate—I don't come to church for this"). It is important for change leaders to listen to feedback, but it is even more important that they not dilute or withdraw the message. Although this is a struggle for the leader who always strives for peace in the congregation, the "creative tension" (see Chapter Seven) that is generated in this stage is healthy and essential to the change process.

Creating urgency does not end when Stage 3 begins. However, a steady and prolonged diet of urgency can be a problem if the congregation does not sense that positive steps are being taken. Throughout the change process, it will be necessary to reassess current reality and to provide new information to the congregation. Regularly highlighting the gap between current reality and God's ideal for his church keeps the change process moving at the optimum speed.

Stage 3: Establishing the Vision Community

Transforming an established congregation, particularly one that is large or old, is a daunting undertaking. It cannot be accomplished without God and it should not be attempted as a solo enterprise of the pastor. The complexity of change and the need to mobilize the full giftedness of the body requires that a group of staff and lay leaders coalesce around the future direction of the church. The purpose of Stage 3 is to establish this group, which we call the *vision community.*

The *vision community* is a diverse group of key members who become a committed and trusting community in order to discern and implement God's vision for the congregation. The vision community should be a part of the change process from beginning to end. Its members must become personally prepared, understand and clearly feel the sense of urgency, and agree that change is needed. They will help in discerning and shaping the vision, in communicating with the broader congregation, and in designing and carrying out the implementation of specific action plans. Jesus' disciples were clearly his vision community. They virtually lived together for three years!

The term *vision community* has been selected carefully and intentionally. The group's central focus will be God's vision for their church.

They should have a burning passion for seeking God's will and for helping the church become all God intends it to be. They should also have the capacity and willingness to experience community together—to develop care and trust that will sustain them through the change process. This is not a committee or task force. Those terms carry specific connotations for most congregations. The connotation might be "business as usual" or "a special group to rubber stamp the pastor's latest project" or "the people who are going to tell us we need a capital fundraising drive." Any name for this group that leads to a misunderstanding of the importance and distinctiveness of its role is a mistake.

The vision community does not diminish the pastor's authority or responsibility. The relationship between the vision community and pastor must be individually negotiated within the context of the specific church's culture and decision-making processes. In most cases, the pastor will clearly be the group's leader. Sometimes, the pastor will function as a peer and the formal leadership role will be filled by a layperson. In all cases the group should be community for the pastor and other paid staff members as well as for each other. The mutual support and encouragement that can be offered by and through this group is important in the ongoing process.

We are often asked at this stage, "Why do we have to go to all this effort?" The answer is related to the dynamics and complexity of change. A low level of effort, as is typical of a task-force approach, is only appropriate for generating a low degree of change. If the radical transformation of a congregation is at stake, a different approach with a much deeper level of commitment is required. The right collection of individuals, knitted together by the Holy Spirit at a deep heart level, must invest heavily in each other and in the process from start to finish.

Who are the right individuals? Ultimately, this is a matter of prayer, careful consideration, and church polity. In some cases, an existing group (board of elders, session, deacons) may form the vision community. In most churches, however, this will be a newly created group. The following suggestions describe the characteristics of vision community membership that provide the best results:

- Diversity reflecting the make-up of the congregation. Dimensions that might be considered in establishing the right diversity are age, gender, ethnicity, length of membership, and representation of key ministries.

- Standing in the congregation. Vision community membership is not limited to individuals currently in formal leadership roles, but those who serve should be respected for their wisdom, maturity, influence, and fair-mindedness.

- Spiritual maturity. This is essential to contribute to discernment and understanding of God's will for the church. This is generally not an assignment for new believers.

- Ability to make a meaningful contribution. Each member of the vision community should be willing and able to share his or her unique perspective and gifts.

- Willing to support the right changes. A fine balance needs to be found at this point. Some church members may meet the above qualifications but are perpetual naysayers—never in favor of a new recommendation, no matter what the basis or supporting facts. At the other extreme are those who always vote with the pastor. Neither of these is an ideal candidate for the vision community.

- Appropriate staff representation. The pastor should always be part of the vision community. In multistaff churches, other ministerial staff should also be included as long as they do not dominate the process. In very large churches, the need for balance may limit the staff to a few individuals representing different ministries or functions.

How many members should the vision community include? Although there are many feasible approaches, we recommend about 10 percent of the average attendance but no more than about twenty-five members. Even at twenty-five, discussion can become very cumbersome. It is generally better to err on the large side and include many different constituencies rather than exclude a key group. In small congregations, it is possible to do the work of the vision community through a series of open meetings as long as a core group commits to the process.

The leadership of the Sand Island Community Church knew that they faced some major decisions. Growth and demographics shifts in the congregation were changing the eighty-year-old church and were straining the capacities of its physical facilities. The church's board decided to follow a formal change process and to create a vision community. The selection of members for the vision community was not taken lightly. No one was asked to serve until considerable time had been spent in prayer about the decision. Danny Newsome, the pastor, spent a great deal of time with the board deciding how to obtain a representative group.

The final composition of the vision community included staff members and lay leaders. It included men and women representing a wide age range, people whose homes were on the island and the mainland, year-round and seasonal ("snowbird") residents, longtime and newer members, and participants in both contemporary and traditional worship services. Those who formed the group committed to attend a vision community retreat and to make a significant, ongoing investment of their time. The three-day retreat focused on understanding God's vision for the church. But a great deal of time was spent in worship and in building a sense of community that would last long after the retreat.

One of the defining moments of the weekend came after considerable effort had been expended to refine and build consensus around an initial vision statement. Arthur, one of the older members, said, "I'm not ready to agree with this statement and the substantial changes that it implies." Even though the rest of the group was ready to move forward, the deep trust and respect that had been established allowed the vision community to honestly and openly deal with his concerns. They recognized that Arthur represented a significant segment of the congregation. For his part, Arthur made it clear that he was not unequivocally against the vision, but that he needed more information first. In this moment, rules about respecting each other's opinions and deciding by consensus were brought to life. Both the final decision and the sense of community that resulted were much stronger.

Suggested Actions to Foster Change

Establishing a vision community involves much more than asking the church's nominating committee to select a representative group of leaders to approve the pastor's vision. From selection through the group's initial meetings, each step should be given adequate consideration, time, and prayer.

Spend Time in Selection Process

The vision community should be selected and approved in accordance with the church's constitution, bylaws, or other established procedures. This is not the time to create conflict by circumventing the rules. It is appropriate, however, for the pastor to spend time with the group that is charged with making the selection to help them understand the role and desired make-up of the group. The pastor should also encourage that time be allowed for prayer and careful consideration. In many churches, the pastor may be allowed to make suggestions for specific members. Even though additional persons can be added later, the best community building occurs when the entire team is together from the start.

Emphasize the Importance of Diversity and Cross-Representation

The vision community should reflect the overall congregation. Widespread change, by definition, affects everyone in the congregation. If the vision community seems to be skewed in its makeup or lacks representation from a particular segment of the church, its decisions are more likely to be criticized and second-guessed as biased or unfair. A good mix avoids this potential problem and provides representatives to help in subsequent communications.

To place these first two actions into proper perspective, imagine a churchwide meeting several months down the road. The subject of the meeting is a final discussion and vote on a significant change. When the pastor recognizes each member of the vision community, what will be going through the minds of the other church members? If many are thinking, "How were they chosen?" or "Looks like the ministers hand-picked the group," or "I don't see anyone who shares my views," the process will suffer a serious setback. The change may be approved, but it may fall far short of an enthusiastic reception. The preferred reactions are "They've really tried to be fair and open about this" or "I can trust this person's opinion." Envisioning this scenario in advance is useful during the selection process.

Address Decision Making and Leadership Issues Up Front

Like most groups, the vision community will function better with a specific set of ground rules and a clear, shared purpose. We refer to these as the vision community's *shared values*. Shared values provide the framework that will guide the vision community's decision making.

Agree on shared values at the outset. Many congregations have an unspoken set of values and rules that will take over if shared values are not explicitly discussed. Seeking consensus in all key decisions might be a desirable shared value. But without explicit agreement, vision community members may assume that "majority votes" will settle decisions. Voting is not wrong, but it does not lend itself to the widespread commitment that is needed. Other unspoken values that often filter into the decision-making process in established congregations are tradition ("We've always done it that way"), finances ("We can't afford that"), self-preservation ("How does that help keep the doors open"), risk avoidance ("What happens if we fail"), and incrementalism ("If we work harder on existing programs, maybe attendance will increase 5 percent"). In addition to consensus, other values to be considered include revelation, innovation, and diversity. When shared values are not adopted early, lack of agreement on the process is likely to emerge at the first contentious point.

Provide Training Where Needed

Each vision community brings a unique set of skills and backgrounds into the first meeting. Training is one of the important ways for vision community members to develop a shared perspective and to learn to work together from a common starting point. The Congregational Transformation Model can be used in this process. Also important is identifying any significant deficiencies or dysfunctional behaviors that could hamper the group's ability to accomplish its task. A tool that helps identify personal conflict styles can be helpful. *Discovering Your Conflict Management Style* (Leas, 1997) is an excellent resource on this subject. Congregations with few leaders may benefit from providing leadership training at this early juncture.

Another way in which community is strengthened is through shared experiences. Vision community members will have the church as one point in common, but it is beneficial to provide other experiences relating to their specific task. Attendance at a conference (for instance, the Purpose Driven Church Conference, Willow Creek Leadership Conference), studying a book on change in churches, visiting other churches, or following a common Bible study are ways of doing this.

Take the Time to Build Community

As in the previous two stages of the change process, it is tempting to rush ahead into vision development or even problem-solving actions. Community building and seeking God's direction take time and should not be set to a rigid schedule. The vision community will comprise highly capable individuals who have many other responsibilities. They will already know enough to be concerned about the church and anxious to move ahead. Members will ask for a meeting agenda and will want to know the overall schedule for the process. Give them a draft agenda, but explain why this might change. Help them take ownership of the process, not for the purpose of keeping it on track but so that the real objectives can be accomplished.

Remember, building community takes time. This is not something that is done up front and then forgotten. A retreat at the beginning of the process is an ideal opportunity for initiating the community-building process and for developing specific skills with the group. Even if a retreat is possible, each meeting of the vision community should include elements that will allow for nurturing trust-based relationships. Times of worship, corporate and intercessory prayer, sharing of concerns, and small-group or team-building exercises can be used to accomplish this end.

Allow Members of the Vision Community to Describe Their Aspirations

One of the ways of building community and creating consensus around a vision is for individual members of the vision community to describe their hopes and aspirations for the church. This does not constrain the scope of the ultimate vision, but it can be an encouraging and revealing exercise that challenges the group to be open to God's desires. Such an exercise strengthens relationships, helps shape the vision, and encourages individual members that their input is important to the process.

A simple question such as "Describe a current or potential ministry to which you would be willing to make a deep, long-term commitment" can open this process for all to participate. When a vision community member expresses a passion for latchkey kids from the local school, she reveals her heart for the church. When another member concurs, an important bond forms. When they both can see how this ministry fits into a vision of ministering to the needs of families in their community, they move much closer to full commitment.

The Benefits of Establishing a Vision Community

No one should attempt congregational transformation as a solo effort. A vision community can play a critical role throughout the transformational effort. Unlike a typical committee, a vision community will

- Truly coalesce around the vision with a high level of commitment to God's leadership, to the church, and to each other.

- Engage in a genuinely collaborative process of discernment and decision making that exceeds the best efforts of a single person or a committee.

- Serve as a critical conduit for getting information out to the congregation and for gathering feedback. Many church members find it easier to ask questions and to offer honest comments to a peer than to the pastor.

- Become a large, trained implementation team that is in place and ready to get started once the vision has been discerned.

Building a vision community was one key to the turnaround of Glenwood Community Church, whose conflict and decline was described in the beginning of this chapter. Pastor Russ Osterman continued to seek opportunities to learn about Saddleback and Willow Creek Community Church. From 1992 to 1996, he took various groups, eighty people in all, with him to Willow Creek's Church Leadership Conference. In 1993, the church began to recover and to effectively reach unchurched people in its community. By 1998, the church was averaging fifty baptisms per year and 635 in attendance. "Being in this setting [Willow Creek] with a large group of Christians whose passion was to reach lost people accelerated the development of a leadership team who could see where I was trying to take the church," says Osterman. From the eighty who have attended Willow Creek, approximately twenty now serve as Glenwood's vision community.

Key Challenge in Establishing the Vision Community

Creating an environment in which challenge and diversity leads to genuine collaboration and commitment.

Selecting the members and beginning to build community is the final groundwork stage. The formation of community continues within the context of discerning and articulating God's vision for the church. In fact, the work of forming and reinforcing the vision community is ongoing. But once the conditions are right—as evidenced by the composition and spirit of the group—it is time to move toward a clear understanding of how God desires to lead the congregation.

Chapter 4

Discerning and Communicating the Vision

THE GROUNDWORK is complete. The pastor and other key leaders have spent time in personal preparation, there is a growing and widely shared sense of urgency that it is not acceptable to maintain the status quo, and a small and diverse group of members has formed to lead the change process. But in what direction will they lead? The difference between recognizing a need for change ("What we are doing is not working") and agreeing on the shape and direction of the change is enormous.

The change process ultimately revolves around the clear discernment and articulation of God's vision for the congregation. As we discuss below, vision is preceded by an understanding of *mission* and it is followed by a detailed description of the *visionpath*. In many ways, achieving clarity and consensus around God's vision is the most important part of the change process. Vision should establish an identity for the congregation—what we are, what we are not, and what we expect to become in three to five years. The earlier stages prepare the congregation's leaders for the task of understanding God's vision. The subsequent stages are all a result of following the vision. Discerning the vision (Stage 4) and communicating the vision (Stage 5) are pivotal to the congregation's transformation.

Stage 4: Discerning the Vision and Determining the Visionpath

Words like *mission, vision,* and *visionpath* are used by many secular and Christian writers, but their meanings often vary. In this book, *mission, vision,* and *visionpath* have separate and distinct meanings. All three help describe God's planned future for a congregation, but the level of detail and specificity increases from mission to vision to visionpath (Figure 4.1). As we have already mentioned in Chapter Three, mission is the most general description. It describes God's eternal purpose for the church and is essentially the same for all congregations (even if different words are used). Mission provides the framework and boundaries for vision.

Vision is a clear, shared, and compelling picture of the preferred future to which God is calling the congregation. Peter Senge states, "Visions are exhilarating. They create the spark, the excitement that lifts an organization out of the mundane" (1990, p. 208). The fourth stage in the change process should result in a written *vision statement* that meets this high standard.

Clear, shared, and compelling—each word underscores essential aspects of vision. The vision must be *clear* for the leaders and members of the congregation to understand it and to make sure that their actions are consistent with it. If it does not become *shared*, disunity and misdirected

FIGURE 4.1   Mission, Vision, and Visionpath

	Mission	Vision	Visionpath
Definition	General description of God's eternal purpose for the church	Clear, shared, and compelling picture of the preferred future to which God is calling the congregation	More detailed description of the steps that will be taken to achieve the vision
Length	One or two sentences	Several sentences or paragraphs	Several pages
Time frame	Eternal	3 to 5 years	1 year
Key question	*For what purpose did God establish the church?*	*What is God's specific call for our congregation?*	*How will our congregation achieve God's vision?*
Necessary perspective	Bible	Mission Prayer Discernment Church's context Vision community	Mission & vision Current reality Bodylife (congregation as a system)

actions will deplete the church's energy. A *compelling* vision motivates the congregation to action. Many vision statements become so academic that they fail to create the excitement and enthusiasm necessary for transformation. Any one of these characteristics is difficult to achieve. To genuinely accomplish all three requires discernment of God's vision, persistence, and hard work.

Many efforts to develop a vision fail to generate meaningful change because the final description of God's preferred future is not comprehensive enough. A clear and concise vision statement needs to be accompanied by a more detailed visionpath. *Visionpath* is the next level of detail beyond vision. It explains the meaning and implications of the vision. Vision describes the big picture of where the church is going, and visionpath begins to fill in details of how the church will get there. A vision statement may be several sentences long, and the visionpath may be several paragraphs or pages long.

In this chapter, we will discuss a process for discerning God's mission, vision, and visionpath and for making this future direction clear to the congregation. Our description of the fourth stage will be different from the others, because in this stage we are describing a specific process within the overall change process. There are many approaches for developing a vision statement and even many different definitions for the word. Our recommendations are based on our observations about the effective use of vision in congregational transformation.

Why is so much time and energy invested in vision? Within a church, shouldn't everyone do the right thing (or at least follow the pastor's lead)? The importance of vision cannot be overstated, particularly for churches that desire God's transformation. A congregation can perform many valuable ministries, any of which can serve God. A clear vision facilitates the selection of those that will have the most impact for the Kingdom in the context of a local body of believers.

Vision also plays an important role in the mobilization of the body. The paradigm of a congregation enthusiastically following its pastor simply because of his position is increasingly uncommon. Members may still respect the pastor, but the most effective ministers have strong leadership skills, including the ability to discern and build commitment around a vision. Far too often, the congregation complies with one person's vision. The process described in this book is based on the assumption that achieving God's vision requires the deep commitment of a broad range of individuals.

We also want to firmly and emphatically state that vision, as used in this book, originates from God. There is a difference between *vision* as used in the business world and secular publications and *vision* as described here. The Bible offers many stories of God implanting his vision in human leaders in order to accomplish his purposes. Moses, Samuel, Nehemiah, Paul, Philip, Peter, and many others were directed in important ways by visions from God. Many of the church leaders with whom we have worked have clearly felt that God has given them a specific vision for their ministry and for their church, and has continued to confirm and shape that vision over time.

Discerning and articulating a vision is hard work. Many congregational leaders stumble over this step. Some try to rush through it without spending the time that is necessary to listen to God and to produce clarity. Others recognize the importance of vision and hesitate to move forward out of fear of making a mistake. Still others realize that this stage will involve a public disclosure of some of their deepest thoughts and feelings, and are unwilling to offer this for public examination and criticism. Recognizing the importance of discerning vision and the centrality of God in the process should provide the focus and perspective to move forward.

The Process

Discerning and agreeing on God's mission, vision, and visionpath for a congregation is a multistep process. At the simplest level, mission must be determined before vision, and vision should determine visionpath. But within each of these three major steps are several substeps. Input is sought, prayerful consideration is given, a first draft is written, private feedback leads to revisions, public feedback leads to a final draft, and finally consensus begins to emerge. These steps are shown in Figure 4.2.

Each of these substeps applies to mission, vision, and visionpath. In the Suggested Approaches section we offer a number of ideas that relate to the steps.

Initial *input* may come from the vision community or the entire congregation. It provides a broad base of information before anything is put in writing. In *prayer*, acknowledge that God is at the center of the process and seek his guidance. *First drafts* are usually written by an individual, not by committee, and most often by the senior pastor. *Private feedback* from a trusted advisor can provide a valuable chance to refine and clarify the draft before it is shown to a larger audience. This can also be an important bridge for pastors who are hesitant to risk putting their

FIGURE 4.2   A Process for Discerning Mission, Vision, and Visionpath

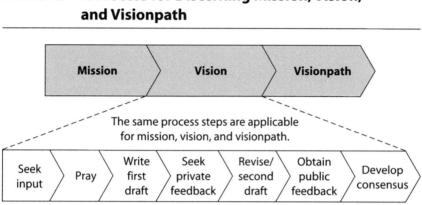

dreams in front of a large group. *Public feedback* usually involves the vision community at first. Their feedback will continue to shape the draft statement until it is ready to be presented to the entire congregation. At this point, a strong *consensus* in support of the congregation's direction should be developing.

The most effective transformation efforts include all of these steps. That is not to say that all of the steps have the same priority or require the same amount of time and energy. It does mean that mission, vision, and visionpath each serve a distinct purpose. And it means that openness, participation, prayer, and a lot of "red ink" are essential elements.

The process that we have described is shaped by several underlying beliefs:

- Vision, as used in this context, originates from God.

- God empowers congregational leaders to discern the vision so that they will have a clear sense of identity and direction concerning their life and ministries.

- The senior pastor plays a central leadership role in the discernment and interpretation of this vision.

- Involvement of a vision community can allow the pastor's vision to merge with the vision of individual lay leaders in a way that builds commitment to a shared vision.

- The entire congregation must ultimately have the opportunity to shape and confirm the vision.

Of these assumptions, the role of the pastor may be the place with the widest range of interpretations among congregations and traditions. We consider the pastor to be God's central servant-leader in the local congregation. In this position, he or she should have God-given insights into the future direction of the congregation. This does not mean that the pastor is the only person to whom God gives such insights, hence the vision community. Our recommended approach involves the pastor and the vision community in a shared discernment process. Some congregations may feel more comfortable, however, if the pastor provides the initial sense of vision, which the vision community modifies and ultimately affirms. There are even processes in which vision communities lead the entire congregation through an assessment, discernment, and planning experience together (Bunker and Alban, 1997).

The best choice for a specific congregation will depend on the church's beliefs and traditions and the personalities of the pastor and key leaders. Whatever the approach, the ultimate objective is the discernment of God's vision for the congregation and a high level of commitment by the pastor and lay leaders. If a deep, *shared* commitment cannot be achieved, true transformation is not possible. (See Chapter Seven for further discussion of commitment.)

The process that we have described cannot be applied dogmatically. As with every stage in the change process, change leaders need to be attuned to the congregation to know when to press ahead and when to slow down. As a general rule, extra time invested in the vision is time well spent. On the other hand, a congregation may already have a clear understanding of mission and may be able to move very quickly through this part of the process. Visionpath may require a modest investment at first but should be revisited and modified frequently.

The Product

The mission, vision, and visionpath can include many elements, and can be written in many different formats. We find the following outline to be effective.

- Vision statement. The first draft should be a few sentences describing the church and the impact that it will have on the community in three to five years.
- Reason for urgency. Why is change necessary? What information about current reality demands that the congregation be willing to change?

This should stand in direct contrast to the vision, and may include statistical information about the church and community, appropriate illustrations and examples, and supportive biblical teachings.

• Clarification of the needed changes. This section should be as detailed and comprehensive as possible. Vague ideas about growth, excellence, or compassion are insufficient. Specific areas to address may include the quality of the congregation's spiritual life, individual ministries and programs, decision-making processes, organization structure, finances, and new ways of thinking.

• Implications of the vision. Once the changes are implemented, what will the end result look like? This section will include a more detailed look at the results that will come from following the vision. These include end results and the underlying drivers, such as behaviors, attitudes, and guiding values. For example, the church may experience a dramatic increase in the number of unchurched people that it reaches as members take prayer more seriously and develop a sense of God's compassion for the lost.

• Call to commitment. Conclude by asking the people of the congregation to join in the clarification and pursuit of this vision.

Since the mission, vision, and visionpath are written in sequence, not all at one time, the product we have just described will not take shape until the end of this stage. It is helpful, though, to have an image of how the various pieces will all come together to describe God's preferred future for the congregation.

Suggested Approaches

In addition to the process and the product, we have several suggestions and techniques that are helpful in developing mission, vision, and visionpath.

Starting from the Right Perspective

Webster defines perspective as "a specific point of view in understanding or judging things or events, especially one that shows them in their true relations to one another." The process of discerning God's vision for a congregation needs to be grounded in his perspective. This means that the change leaders must spend time asking God for guidance and clarity. The process of vision discernment is not an exercise to legitimize a leader's personal ambitions.

A related and helpful approach is Covey's concept of "beginning with the end in mind" (1989). We expand this by encouraging congregational leaders to "start at the endpoint and work back." Said another way, the pastor should start with a clear sense of the congregation's mission and should then ask, "Of all the things this congregation could do over the next three to five years, which ones will help us make the most rapid progress toward the achievement of our mission?" For example, a church that seeks to play an integral role in shaping its community in five years needs to start by learning about the world outside its walls. Where are the gaps between what God intends for that community and what is actually happening? Vision grows and is clarified out of commitments to make measurable progress toward God's ideal.

Far too often, vision is developed by asking "What can be done tomorrow?" and then extending that into the future. This approach has many appeals: it is logical, it is easier to envision, it is less risky, it keeps from stretching the church's resources. The problem is that extrapolation grows out of incremental thinking and leaves little room for God to be at work in the midst of the congregation. If the vision is from God, no matter how big it is, we believe that he will provide the means to achieve it in time. Being open to God's revelation of his preferred future is an essential first step toward discerning his vision.

Find the Right Setting

Drafting the vision statement or visionpath is not something to mark off of a "to do" list in between appointments one afternoon. For the vision to have power in the life of the congregation, it must first and foremost come from the heart of God. A good setting is one way to facilitate this. Setting aside a day to get away, at a retreat center if possible, is an especially good way to shut out the other distractions. The setting should help offset the temptation to "get down to business" right away. Instead, this time should begin with worship, meditation on God's word, confession of sin, and a petition for forgiveness and healing. As this process unfolds, God will call to mind other occasions when he has made his vision clear at a personal and congregational level. When this creative energy begins to flow, it is time to begin an initial draft.

Seek Feedback and Refine the Document

The feedback of a trusted friend can be invaluable as an intermediate step between drafting the vision and sharing it with the vision community. A member of the vision community or a consultant who is involved in the change process can serve in this role. The important characteristics that this person needs to bring are a good personal rapport, prior experience with vision development, and a knack for offering deep and useful insights.

Ask the advisor to honestly answer three questions about the draft of the vision or visionpath. Is it clear? Is it comprehensive? Is it compelling? Once the advisor has had time to read and reflect on the vision and visionpath, spend time together reviewing his or her comments. The notes from this review should be used to create a second draft of the vision and visionpath.

Giving the first draft to someone else and asking for honest feedback is the first risk that must be taken to succeed in this process. Some pastors will be tempted to try to perfect the first draft. Getting a complete set of ideas on paper may take more than the one day described above, but it is better to get feedback from a trusted friend than to continue writing the text in isolation. Even the most meticulous editing and rewriting process is less helpful than the comments that a fresh set of eyes can bring.

Throughout the process, look on feedback as a valuable resource that will improve the result. If the draft is unclear or incomplete, no purpose— other than the protection of the author's fragile ego—is served by leaving it in this state.

Engage the Vision Community in Dialogue About the Vision

Processing a vision statement with the vision community is a critical step in the process. It represents a shift from following the pastor's vision to building a shared vision. Giving the document to the vision community in a spirit of humility and openness is a difficult task for many pastors. One pastor described this part of the process as "giving birth in a room full of people, and then surrendering the baby to the audience's custody, all while worrying that they will not even like the child." Regardless of how much time has been spent in preparation or how cohesive the vision community may be, presentation of the vision will lead to questions and differing opinions. The bigger the dream that God has given to the pastor, the greater the fear that the vision community will respond with astonishment and bewilderment.

Making the transition from the pastor's understanding of God's vision to a genuinely shared vision is delicate. The pastor must be genuine in asking for honest feedback. When the first criticism or alternate suggestion is offered, all of the vision community members will be watching carefully. A defensive reaction will tell them that their feedback is not really wanted. Defensiveness in this setting can come in many varieties—from aggression or aggravation ("Your comment is wrong") to condescension ("If you could see things from where I sit, you would understand") to persuasion ("Yes, but the reason that I think this is important is . . . "). Making people feel rushed is another way to suffocate openness. Any of these reactions will tend to restrain constructive dialogue.

The range of responses to the vision statement can also be confusing or frustrating. One person may see the forest ("Why do you believe we need to go in that direction?") and the next person may be focused on the trees ("I think the third sentence should say 'will' instead of 'can'"). Give some structure to the feedback process. One way of ordering the discussion is to guide the vision community through four questions. Explain all four questions at the outset and ask them to offer their comments at the appropriate time.

1. *What is your overall reaction to the vision and visionpath?* This is a general question to which everyone should respond.

2. *What questions about the meaning of the vision do you have?* This makes sure that everyone has the same understanding of the words that are in front of them.

3. *Are there concepts or ideas that should be added or deleted?* This question focuses on substantive changes in the vision and visionpath.

4. *Are there ways we can say this better?* This focuses on making individual words and phrases as effective as possible. Much of the attention here should be given to editing and distilling the vision statement into its most compact and dynamic form.

It will not be possible to discuss all of these questions in one meeting. In fact, it is valuable to have multiple meetings. This creates "soak time" so that the vision community can reread the words and ask God to speak clearly to them. One natural place to break is after initial comments to the third question have been offered. The vision community can then be instructed to take the document with them for further prayerful consideration. When the vision community reconvenes, the third question can be repeated so that they have a chance to share from their time of consideration.

Once the vision community has had the opportunity to see the draft of the vision and visionpath, pray about it, and offer their comments, a consensus should begin to emerge around the principal elements of the vision. In congregations with a history of distrust or where dramatic change is required, several meetings may be needed to reach this point. One or more members may insist that the best approach is to "just do a better job with the existing programs and ministries and quit trying to change everything." Congregational leaders will have to make the judgment call of when to move forward, keeping in mind that a majority vote is not the same as commitment.

Prepare a Final Draft and Ask for the Vision Community's Affirmation

The pastor should prepare a final draft, incorporating as much of the vision community's feedback as possible without compromising his understanding of God's revelation. In working on this draft, it is particularly helpful to distinguish the vision from the specific words that are used to communicate it. Incorporating suggested words and phrases that do not change the meaning is one way to increase commitment. This is also the time to wrestle with the specific words in the vision statement to make it as clear, concise, and compelling as possible. Before this draft is finished, the pastor should put it aside for a day or two and then reread it, asking one more time if it is a clear and compelling description of the vision that he or she understands God to have for the congregation.

The vision community should be given a copy of this draft and should be requested to prayerfully consider it in preparation for a final discussion. In this discussion, they should answer two questions. Is the vision clear? Is this a vision to which I am willing to commit myself? There is likely to be some additional fine-tuning, but there should not be any significant resistance at this point. If there is opposition, it may be necessary to slow the process and not press for final adoption of the vision statement. Ultimately, the pastor and the vision community need to be in strong agreement that the vision is right and that they are ready to proceed. A vote or other clear step should be taken to signify the vision community's ownership and support of the vision.

Anticipate and Proactively Address Resistance

A vision statement will almost always describe a future that will require change for the congregation. Consequently, the pastor and vision community are certain to encounter opposition in this stage. Even though resistance can come in many forms and from many different directions, it can often be anticipated. Thinking about which parts of the vision are likely to be most controversial, and for which segments of the congregation, is one way to anticipate.

With this awareness, change leaders can develop a specific plan for addressing the issues. This plan might be to slow the process down so that someone can "get on board" or to tailor certain communications to address the specific concerns. The pastor should be attentive to the vision community during the process to see whether one or two might have lingering concerns. As the momentum builds, it is common for someone to silently withdraw rather than be the one dissenting voice. A one-on-one meeting with this person may bring him or her back in the fold and may add a unique insight to the process.

It is not uncommon, however, for one or more persons to withdraw completely as this process unfolds. As consensus emerges around the vision, they realize that they will never be able to genuinely commit to the vision. Even though it is painful, it is important for the vision community to be willing to allow them to leave the group or even to find another congregation where they can continue to serve God. Failure to do so will weaken the vision and will result in more significant challenges down the road. In some congregations, the transformation process stalls out here. They adopt a posture that all must go forward or none will go at all. Some congregations decide that keeping peace among the existing members is more important than discerning and pursuing a clear vision from God.

The alternative to anticipating resistance is to hope that there will be no objections, and then to be surprised when they inevitably arise. When surprise and confrontation mix, however, the result is usually not very pleasant. Since some conflict is unavoidable during vision discernment and transformation, the best course is to manage the conflict proactively and constructively in order to achieve a positive outcome.

The Benefits of Discerning the Vision and Determining the Visionpath

It may be daunting to try to discern and articulate God's vision for a congregation, but the downside of not doing so is even more frightening. By creating a commitment to a shared vision, the pastor and vision community will

- Acknowledge a distinct calling and identity for the church
- Make God's direction for the congregation's future clear and explicit
- Excite and motivate the vision community and the entire congregation
- Provide a framework and basis for making future decisions

Key Challenge in Discerning the Vision and Visionpath

Producing a written description of God's preferred future that is broad and exciting in its direction but clear and explicit in its details.

As a final note, the vision that God reveals is likely to evolve and become clearer over time. The story of the children of Israel's exodus from Egypt shows that God continues to reveal his plans. Neither Moses nor the people understood what would unfold when Moses first confronted Pharaoh after seeing the burning bush. We are all called to be open to God's leadership, to respond even when the pathway to the destination is unclear, and to be prepared for God to reveal more of his plans as the journey continues. In the context of developing a vision, congregations need to be as clear as possible in their understanding of God's vision, but they also must be willing to reexamine the vision throughout the change process.

Stage 5: Communicating the Vision

In the Sermon on the Mount, Jesus tells his followers, "You are the light of the world. A city on a hill cannot be hidden. Neither do people light a lamp and put it under a bowl. Instead they put it on its stand, and it gives light to everyone in the house" (Matthew 5:14–15). Although Jesus was specifically instructing his followers to proclaim the Gospel to a hungry world, the same principle applies to the need to communicate God's vision to the local body of believers.

In one respect, *communication* is an uninterrupted continuation of vision development. But it also represents a major shift in the transformation journey. The fifth stage is where the vision and the overall change process become much more public. The implications of this shift should not be underestimated. Up to this point, much of the effort related to change has been done within the confines of a small group, the vision community. Communication has been done one-on-one and in the context of close relationships. The process has been intentionally structured—in its pace, depth, and repetition—to ensure that any miscommunication or misunderstanding is quickly resolved.

When the entire congregation is brought into the process in Stage 5, communication takes on an entirely different meaning. Our definition of _communicating the vision_ is a comprehensive, intentional, and ongoing set of activities that are undertaken throughout the transformation process to make the vision clear to the congregation. The intent of the communication stage is to generate a high level of _understanding_ and _commitment_ to God's vision for the congregation. Failure to effectively communicate the vision can temporarily stop or even permanently damage the entire transformation process.

John Kotter estimates that undercommunicating the vision by a factor of ten (or even 100 or 1000) is one of the most common mistakes made by organizations that are engaging a change process (1996, p. 9). Our experience is that this mistake is made even more frequently in churches. Rick Warren reinforces this theme when he says, "Vision and purpose must be restated every twenty-six days to keep the church moving in the right direction" (1995, p. 111).

If the vision is this important, why do so many congregations fail at this stage? Why is so much communication about the vision necessary? Why can't the congregation "get it" the first time?

Think again about what happens in Stage 4 as the vision is emerging. When the first draft of a vision statement is presented to the vision community, misunderstanding and even disagreement almost always occur. Members of the vision community have the benefit of careful explanations and multiple opportunities to hear, reflect, and discuss. They have ample opportunities to express doubts and to raise questions.

In the excitement to announce the vision and begin implementation, change leaders often forget that the rest of the congregation has not been a part of the intense dialogue and soul-searching that are a part of discerning and articulating the vision. In forgetting this key fact, they underestimate the amount of communication that will be required. To expect commitment from the congregation without adequate interaction and understanding is unrealistic.

We encourage all congregations to keep this simple truth in mind as they consider how they will communicate the vision that God has implanted in the hearts of the pastor and the vision community. The unavoidable reality is that people only absorb a small portion of what they hear. When communicating with a congregation or any large group, some will not be listening at all, and few if any will be able to hear and understand all that is said. Any communication strategy that is based on a "tell them once and move on" philosophy is sure to fail. This is especially true when the multifaceted nature of the vision is considered. "Unpacking" the richness of the vision for the congregation's understanding will take time and repetition.

If *pace*—the rate at which the new information can be absorbed—is the first factor that should dictate the communication strategy, then *personality* is the second. People learn in different ways. A single communication may be extremely effective for some members but completely miss the mark for others. A written vision statement in a newsletter will form a lasting impression and will allow one person to mull it over in their mind. Verbal delivery, with the emotion and illustrations that accompany it, will create a strong image for others. People also hear through different "filters" at different times. This means that an ongoing communication process is important. Today, I may have a deep concern about an unchurched friend. This leads me to focus on the part of the vision that addresses evangelism. A year from now, the same friend's needs for discipleship may result in my hearing the same vision in a completely different light.

Priority is the third reality that must be considered in communications. Even if everyone heard and understood the entire vision the first time, repetition signals priority. Many congregations develop effective communication strategies that culminate in a vote to approve the vision. Their follow-up communication consists of adding the vision statement as a small footnote in the church's written materials and then they shift to other information. When this happens, members will subconsciously relegate the vision and the entire change process to the "program of the month" heap. Frequency of communication is a direct indication of importance. Therefore, repetition of the vision throughout the change process is essential.

Effective communication is based on an explicit recognition of all these factors. It blends creativity, repetition, and a strong awareness of the audience to deliver a message with maximum impact. Jesus was a master communicator. He taught his followers with parables, practical and patient explanations, Old Testament prophecies, and actions. He repeated his central themes over and over without using the exact same words. Christ knew that we would not fully grasp his message immediately upon hearing it, and we should strive to have the same patience and persistence with today's listeners.

Suggested Actions to Foster Change

How do change leaders create a high level of understanding and commitment to the vision? What does a comprehensive, intentional, and ongoing communication strategy look like? As with all of the stages, the answer will be unique to each individual congregation. Some of the common principles and examples of effective strategies for communicating the vision are as follows.

Develop an Explicit Communication Strategy

Communication of the vision should not be left to chance. After the vision and visionpath are agreed on and put into writing, the vision community should develop a communication strategy. The strategy should address how communication will be done, who will be responsible, and what the timing will be. Feedback and evaluation of the effectiveness of communications should also be an explicit part of the strategy. Those responsible for communications need to know whether the congregation is understanding and getting excited about the vision. Without feedback, they will miss the opportunity to improve their approach. A template for communication strategies is included in the workbook.

Communication objectives will change over time, and change leaders need to be prepared to change the strategy accordingly. The initial goal is to achieve a basic understanding and acceptance of the vision across the congregation. Explanation, interpretation, and response to questions will play a key role when the vision is new. The ultimate objective of most initial communication strategies is a formal decision by the congregation to affirm the vision. Nothing is wrong with this focus—the initial steps to communicate are very important. But the vision community should develop a new communication strategy after the congregational decision. This strategy might be focused on a specific aspect of the vision that is not clearly understood or a deeper recognition of the vision's implications. Any ongoing communication strategy should be based on the need for repetition and should address how new members will be exposed to the vision. Just as the initial strategy targets an affirmative vote, subsequent communications should be designed to build an ever-growing level of commitment.

Be Creative in Communications

Communicating the vision is a comprehensive set of activities. It is not limited to sermons and newsletters, where many congregations stop in their communication strategies. Think of as many different ways to communicate the vision as possible. In addition to the two standards listed above, some of the successful ways to communicate include detailed "white papers" (typically more than what can be put in a newsletter), small discussion groups, videos, specially composed music, and dramas.

Creative refers to more than the form of communication—it also entails how the same message is variously delivered. Clearly explaining a new program (or a change in an existing program) as a result of the vision is effective communication. Likewise, recognizing an individual or group's work in one aspect of the church's life and linking this directly to the vision reinforces the message in a new way. Keeping the vision community involved in planning communications will spur creativity as they have a chance to interact and to build on one another's ideas.

Enlist the Entire Vision Community

Responsibility for each element of communication should be clearly specified. If the burden always falls on the same one or two people (maybe the pastor and another staff person or key lay leader), the desired impact and comprehension will be impossible to achieve across the congregation. The entire vision community should have an active role in communicating the vision. Beyond the obvious advantage of sharing the task, enlisting the vision community in the process allows the congregation to hear about the vision from a respected peer. This can greatly increase the likelihood and pace of acceptance. It also creates a natural pathway for any questions that members may have about the vision.

One effective approach is to set up a number of small group meetings (in homes, if possible) in which different vision community members will present the vision and host a time of question and answer. In whatever setting and format they are involved, the use of various vision community members adds an important dimension to communications.

The vision is offered from different perspectives but with a strong consensus around its necessity and its ultimate meaning.

Develop Terms, Phrases, and Analogies That Have Special Meaning for Your Congregation

Why do pastors use illustrations in their sermons? They use them because people remember the illustrations far more easily than the exegesis. The same principle applies to the communication of the vision. An illustration or a coined phrase may require explanation the first time that it is used, but it can become a powerful kind of shorthand for helping the congregation remember and describe the vision. It is not a coincidence that some of the most successful churches in America today make liberal use of catchy phrases. "Fully devoted followers of Christ," "Saddleback Sam," "Unchurched Harry and Mary," and other word images have become well known in many evangelical circles because of how they motivate and teach a local congregation.

Change leaders who do not have a talent for crafting clever language can research what others have done and ask for permission to use their work. One of the masters in this area is Rick Warren, pastor of Saddleback Community Church, who gives liberal permission to other church leaders to borrow and adapt the many different descriptors that he and his church have developed over the years.

Repeat, Repeat, Repeat

The last time that a church member was aggravated because he or she "didn't know anything about" a well-publicized congregational event is probably a fresh memory for most of us. Repetition is an essential ingredient in the communication strategy. Repetition does not, however, mean saying the same words over and over. The best communicators continually find fresh ways to present the vision. They do not say, "Listen closely while I explain the vision one more time." And yet the central themes of the vision permeate their message.

The church leader who assumes that the vision has been understood and internalized after the initial round of communication is asking for trouble. The problems of insufficient communication may not become evident until later in the transformation process. It is not unusual for a new vision to be overwhelmingly approved by the congregation, only to see the launch of new initiatives flounder for lack of support. Pastors will contend that they have too much to say to devote so much of their communication to repetition of the vision. Our response is that the effective articulation of God's vision, and how the congregation will achieve it, are as important as any message that the pastor may have to offer.

Seek Feedback on the Vision

The communication stage is one of several points in the change process where feedback is essential. Even if the communication strategy has been thoughtfully designed and the pastor is a powerful communicator, it is impossible to predict exactly how the message will be heard and interpreted. The need to build a high level of understanding and commitment to the vision is too important for anyone to assume blindly that their strategy has been successful. Using the vision community as informal listening points, conducting a survey, and asking (genuinely) for feedback can indicate the effectiveness of the message. If the results are negative, this does not necessarily mean that the vision is wrong, but it does suggest that more time should be spent in this stage and that the communication strategy should be modified.

The Benefits of Communicating the Vision

The benefits of communicating may be clarified best by highlighting the risks of not communicating. Failure to communicate the vision effectively will result in the overall transformation process being delayed, diffused, or derailed. It can also result in significant conflict if the leadership pushes the process forward despite insufficient communication. Many churches have been deeply hurt and many pastors bear the scars of the failure to communicate adequately. Keep these dangers in mind in the face of the temptation to shortcut this stage.

Effective communication of the vision

- Creates clear understanding and increases the likelihood of deep commitment to the vision

- Establishes a broad base of members who will actively support the transformation process

- Gives a strong signal to the congregation that things are going to be different

- Promotes a more systematic way of looking at the activities and ministries by relating everything to the vision

- Answers the what, why, and how questions on members' minds, thereby reducing their fear of and resistance to change
- Helps individual members to see clearly how they can (or do) support the congregation's future

Key Challenge in Communicating the Vision

Finding creative ways that enable the entire congregation to thoroughly understand God's vision for their future and its implications.

Knowing that communication has been adequate and effective is both easy and difficult. The easy part comes when the votes are counted and the vision is approved by the congregation. But the real indicator will be how individual members show their commitment in the months and years ahead.

Chapter 5

Achieving and Maintaining Widespread Impact

LIKE A MOVIE director who has spent hours on casting, set design, and script revisions, the final three stages of the change process are the call for "Action!" The public may think that the on-screen image is all that matters, but the director knows the importance of the behind-the-scenes work. In many ways, the final three stages of the change process are a single "on-camera" activity. Showing them as three parts clarifies and emphasizes critical concepts, obstacles, and transitions. Stage 6 deals with empowerment of the vision community and other key leaders who will be responsible for specific actions related to the vision. Stage 7 focuses on the nuts and bolts of implementation, including the complexities of multiple concurrent initiatives and the need for making continuous adjustments. Stage 8 is a reminder that visions have to be revisited and refreshed, that a single set of implementation initiatives will never be sufficient to achieve the vision, and that transformation is really a continuous, iterative process.

Continuing with the movie analogy, we can compare the last three stages of the change process to roles in producing the film. Stage 6, empowerment, is closely related to the roles played by the director, producer, and casting director. They may never appear on camera, but they are always intimately involved in achieving the desired result. They assign roles, both to actors and to the many different support personnel. When problems arise on the set, the director and producer are the ones who bring about resolution so that filming can continue. So it is with Stage 6: The action may be off-camera but it affects everything else. Stage 7 is analogous to the lead roles. These are the parts that require extra time and attention before filming to learn accents and get a feel for the historical context. The actors and actresses playing these characters are the ones the audience talks about after seeing the film. And so the key priorities in Stage 7 become the focal points of the change process. Stage 8 involves the supporting cast, the special effects, the soundtrack—everything else that contributes to the audience's experience in viewing the movie. If these parts are not aligned with the lead characters, the movie cannot be successful. In the change process, the rest of the congregation must become aligned with the vision and the new direction.

Two of the most successful movies in recent years have been *Titanic* and *Saving Private Ryan*. Both of these movies illustrate the interwoven relationship between the final three stages of the change process. When reminded of these films, our first thought may be of the stars—Leonardo Di Caprio, Kate Winslett, Tom Hanks. And each turned in brilliant acting performances. But without the many decisions made by James Cameron and Steven Spielberg, the movies would have been much less powerful. Imagine the scenes in the final moments before the *Titanic* sank without the precise execution of the dozens of small parts, or what *Saving Private Ryan* might have been like if the powerful sound and special effects during the Normandy landing had not worked exactly right. In the change process, congregations inevitably focus on a few major new priorities. But if the empowerment and alignment stages are not done with equal intentionality and effectiveness, the process will fall short of the mark.

Stage 6: Empowering Change Leaders

Our definition of *empowerment*, as practiced most effectively in leading congregations, consists of two equally important elements: (1) establishing a new model for leadership within the congregation and (2) removing the obstacles that would prevent leaders from serving effectively. Too many churches and church leaders attempt implementation without empowerment. That is why Stage 6 (empowerment) is shown before Stage 7 (implementation), even though the two are essentially concurrent. Implementation entails the specific and visible actions taken to make the vision a reality. Empowerment is the set of enabling tasks that make these actions possible.

The new leadership model involves broadening the leadership base in the congregation beyond the pastor and a few lay leaders. This requires authorizing and trusting others to take on major responsibilities, but it also means adopting a new mindset in the mobilization and training of new leaders. Empowerment is also about removing obstacles that these new leaders face. The more dramatic the change, the more obstacles will be encountered. If these obstacles are not dealt with in a proactive manner, they will undermine the entire process.

Consider a congregation that has identified a segment of unchurched people in its community and is committed to reaching them as a part of its vision. The church's visionpath (how they will achieve the vision) includes the creation of a contemporary worship service in addition to its traditional 11:00 A.M. service. The pastor recognizes that neither he nor the ministerial staff has the time or the skills to undertake this initiative successfully. Identifying members of the congregation who have the passion and skills and allowing them to be responsible for the new worship is a first step of empowerment. Genuine empowerment is demonstrated when the newly appointed worship leader is allowed to lead the decision-making process, with input from the pastor and others on the leadership team. This may include setting the time for the worship service (based on an understanding of how to best reach the target audience), assembling the rest of the team for this service, modifying the church's budget so that publicity and other related actions can be funded, and redesigning the way in which visitors are identified and contacted.

Many things stand in the way of empowerment. In some churches, it is a fear of delegation because "no one else will do it right." Others have a culture in which the paid staff is expected to do all the work. It is not easy to be a competent, paid minister and not worry about surrendering control. In many cases, this orientation is taught in seminary, expected by the congregation, modeled by other pastors, and confirmed by previous (disastrous) experiences. To those who urge delegation, it is easy to respond, "I'm the one with the full-time job on the line." Still others feel guilty about asking laypeople to help shoulder the burden of leadership. Yet broadening the leadership base and authorizing others to take responsibility is the only way to make adequate progress in the change process. The pastor, even with a handful of other staff members and key leaders, simply cannot do all the tasks that face a transforming congregation.

Even with the right leaders, the congregation's structures and procedures can be major barriers to the change process. These can include the formal organization structure for staff and committees; job descriptions; constitution, bylaws, and other rules (written and unwritten) for decision making; information systems; and financial procedures. Unwritten (tacit) norms are often the most powerful.

The existing structures and procedures, if not carefully examined and reshaped, can undermine a specific change initiative before it ever gets off the ground. A staggered, multiple committee approval process that takes several months to culminate makes it impossible to be flexible and responsive. Measurement of results may be impossible because of how information is gathered and reported. A report that does not show the number of visitors who return to the church or that fails to distinguish transfer members from new Christians is of little value in supporting a vision of reaching the unchurched. Each of these is an example of how structures can hinder effective pursuit of the vision. In the example of contemporary worship, it would be absurd to ask a committed and respected layperson to lead this initiative and then to hamstring the effort by not making money, other people, and information available. Unfortunately, too many change efforts build just this sort of fatal flaw into their design.

As important as empowerment is, it also has a dangerous side. Church leaders should never use the empowerment stage of the process as an excuse for making indiscriminate changes in the current structure. Removal of barriers is important, but the change process is a long journey with many obstacles along the route. It is not necessary to clear the entire route before the journey ever begins. In fact, enormous energy can be expended in removing the remote obstacles at the expense of initial progress. Wise leaders determine which obstacles need to be moved immediately and which are inconsequential to current efforts, which are easy to overcome and which should be circumvented or ignored.

A committee structure that always seems to impede key decisions may be a major concern to change leaders. Before beginning an all-out effort to change the governance structure, they should pause and reflect. Is the committee system an obstacle to achieving the vision? Is it a barrier to the *current* priorities in the visionpath? Even if the answer to the first question is clearly "Yes!" a negative answer to the latter suggests that this battle should be postponed. And even if the system stands in the way of current priorities, the leaders should recognize the cost of the changes and evaluate other alternatives before proceeding. Determining when sufficient progress can be made within the current structure and when the cost (in terms of time and trust) is too great to justify wholesale change is a sign of a wise leader.

Steve Norris, the senior minister of University Church, could not remember any time in his eight-year tenure when the congregation had been so enthusiastic. Their nine-month effort to seek God's vision for the church had led to a clear sense of direction. In retrospect it seemed obvious that God would want them to refocus their efforts on reaching out to the large college campus at their doorstep. Yet Steve recognized that this would require many changes, and that the time spent in prayerful consideration of God's will had built a much deeper level of commitment than could have been achieved otherwise.

Steve was looking forward to his Tuesday morning breakfast meeting with Grace Collins, the church's volunteer minister of students. The vision community had asked them to recommend specific initiatives for restarting the college ministry. Grace was a creative and energetic person, and he knew that she would come to their first meeting full of great ideas.

Grace described an exciting opportunity and several concrete ideas for reaching out to the students. Then she explained the dilemma. "We have just approved our annual budget, and we only have $200 for college ministries. I need at least $1,000 to get started. Under our current rules, I won't have the funds we need for almost a year."

Over the course of several meetings, Steve and Grace discussed their options and limitations. Even though the majority of the congregation supported the vision and the new focus on the college ministry, the commitment was not unanimous. A number of the older members were wary of change. Furthermore, it did not seem feasible to "fix" the budget process. A financial scandal fourteen years earlier had left some of these same members suspicious any time that change involved handling the finances differently.

Ultimately, Steve and Grace found a creative way to revise the original recommendations into a less expensive option. They still needed additional funding but were able to use a designated account that had been set up years earlier for student work. In doing so, University Church was able to begin following its vision without expending energy in unnecessary conflict.

Empowerment does not require that everything be fixed at once. It is about focusing on the vision, finding the right people to do the job, and then removing the obstacles that stand directly in their path.

Christ gives us the ultimate example of empowerment. At the time of his betrayal and arrest, his vision community (the eleven remaining disciples) hardly seemed prepared for the awesome responsibility that would follow. (They were certainly less prepared than many lay leaders in today's church.) They were confused as to who he was, still clung to old concepts of the Messiah, fell asleep, and ran away in fear. Jesus showed them by example how to remove the obstacles that would stand in their way—a deeply embedded, legalistic mental model of "how religion was done," the iron-fisted grip of the religious establishment, and an exclusive attitude toward those of non-Jewish backgrounds. His example should challenge all of us to empower other leaders and to facilitate change by removing the real barriers that stand in the way.

Suggested Actions for Fostering Change

Empowerment must address the twin issues of the congregation's leadership model and the barriers to change that may exist. Each congregation will need to develop specific plans for empowerment that recognize and address both of these concerns. Some possible elements to include in these plans are as follows.

Be in the Business of Cultivating Leaders

Empowerment is possible only if capable individuals are available to accept leadership assignments. Successful corporations invest heavily in recruiting, training, tracking, mentoring, and managing men and women so that a pool of executives is always available. Unfortunately, most churches fall far short in this area. Existing leaders are usually overworked, and potential leaders are routinely "thrown to the wolves" with little or no training or support. Approaches to identify and prepare promising candidates are rare. God gives the spiritual gifts that the body needs, but they still need to be discovered and nurtured within a local church. Any investment that makes leadership cultivation less haphazard will have enormous payback.

Training can take many forms. Some training will be specific to a potential leader's upcoming assignment. It may be provided by the church or through participation in an outside conference. Some congregations use an apprenticeship or leader-in-training model to cultivate new leaders for their small groups. We have also seen many benefits when leaders participate in more general training at a churchwide level. For example, teaching the eight-stage change process can increase the commitment and capability of the leadership group. A regular (monthly) leadership meeting is often effective for training, communication, and reinforcement of the vision, and it provides another place where potential leaders can "test the water."

Establish a Permission-Giving Culture

A permission-giving culture encourages individual leaders within the congregation to take initiative, take risks, and experiment. The opposite of a permission-giving culture is not one that denies permission, it is one that controls, second guesses, and micromanages every decision. The permission-giving culture allows a college ministry leader to redesign the Bible study time and format, not demand that "Sunday School always uses our denominational literature and it always begins at 9:30." The best way to create this culture is for the pastor or other change leaders to create a buffer zone around the first few initiatives. This is the extra layer of protection that makes it acceptable to try and "fail," that deflects inappropriate criticism away from those who are leading the new effort, and that ensures that needed resources are available. The authority and support that these leaders receive demonstrates the desired culture by example.

Create Accountability

A permission-giving culture does not mean that accountability is lost. A central tenet of our leadership model is that specific individuals in the congregation will be responsible for change initiatives and that they will act out of a clear understanding of the church's vision. For their specific assignment, the visionpath and related goals must be clear and must guide their efforts. When possible, particularly in the early stages of the change process, these individuals should be members of the vision community. This increases the likelihood that specific actions will be in alignment with the spirit and intent of the vision. It is not easy to balance accountability and autonomy, but both are needed to propel the change process forward.

Understand the Current Structures

Structure and procedure cannot be changed until they have been identified and the ways in which they block implementation of the vision have been understood. Some, such as financial reporting and decision-making processes, exist in every church. Others are unique to the local congregation. The accompanying workbook provides a tool for assessing these systems.

Describing the real structures is important if meaningful decisions are to be made. For example, the bylaws may state that an out-of-budget expenditure requires approval by the Finance Committee and the Elder Board. In reality, however, the Finance Committee meets only once a month and consistently tables any new request until the next meeting. The result is a minimum of three months until the expenditure can be made. It is only by accurately describing how these structures actually work that the need for change can be evaluated and the specific changes can be implemented.

Determine Which Changes Are Needed Based on Current Priorities

Once structures and procedures have been identified, the necessary changes can be made. Remember that not all barriers need to be removed for the change process to get under way, and the appropriate action may be to modify a procedure rather than eliminating or replacing it. Changes may be formal, informal, or somewhere in between. Formal changes normally require the official approval of the church or a governing body. Giving more autonomy to the pastor, changing financial procedures, or modifying how leadership positions are filled are typically formal system changes. An informal change would be to speed up the expenditure decision cited above. It does not require official approval, but it does require doing things differently. There are also a host of changes that may fall in between the formal and informal. For example, Bible study leaders may be given the freedom to select their own curriculum (rather than having this done by a paid staff member). Or the attendance reports may be changed to capture more information. These changes require formal steps, but would not typically require an official decision.

Develop Prototypes and Descriptions of the Ideal Systems

Part of the difficulty in changing structures is caused by outright resistance—the mentality that "we've always done it that way." But awareness and communication can be another barrier—congregations may have no idea what change is needed or why. Describing and prototyping the preferred system is one of the best ways to help members of the congregation visualize the alternative. If effective outreach requires more information, such as visitation frequency, follow-up contact, date of last attendance, and small group assignment, this must be clearly stated. Developing a sample table showing the preferred information is especially helpful.

Don't Break the Rules

In the process of rewriting the rules, the congregation's leaders must not break the rules. Although this may seem paradoxical, it is an important message. In the early stages of empowerment and implementation, the entire change process is hanging in the balance. If the formal rules are broken in the haste to "make something happen," those who are not on board with the new vision will gain ammunition for their resistance. For example, it may seem imperative to rewrite the job descriptions of staff members to facilitate the change process. If this is the responsibility of the personnel committee, they must be included, even if this means delays. Failure to work within the official rules to bring about change is a clear case of being penny-wise and pound-foolish. It will lead to unnecessary conflict and ultimately cause even lengthier delays in the process.

The Benefits of Empowering Change Leaders

The immediate and long-term benefits of empowerment are integral to the change process. Empowerment, including the delegation of responsibility and the removal of barriers, is essential because it

- Creates a large enough leadership base to truly accomplish the change process. Deep, systemic change in a congregation can never be accomplished solely by the pastor.
- Makes the long-term transformation much more efficient. Each structure and procedure that is brought in line with the vision adds direct support to the process.
- Accelerates the change process.
- Takes advantage of the greatest resource that the pastor has at this point in the process—the commitment and enthusiasm of the vision community.
- Avoids the frustration of initiatives that are doomed before they ever begin because of insurmountable barriers.
- Reinforces the vision.

Key Challenge in Empowering the Vision Community

Cultivating a broader base of committed leaders and removing the barriers that would prevent them from serving effectively.

Empowerment is essential. But it needs to be linked with the implementation of high-leverage initiatives that flow out of the vision.

Stage 7: Implementing the Vision

The normal leadership response to a declining congregation is to "start doing something." It is not a coincidence that the implementation stage does not occur until the change process is three-fourths complete. Implementation—without the direction provided by vision, without the support provided by a vision community, without the enabling of empowerment—cannot be done effectively any earlier in the process. If it is done earlier, it is just as likely to be a catalyst for life-threatening conflict as for life-giving change.

We define *implementation* as a specific set of coordinated, high-leverage initiatives that move the congregation toward realization of God's vision. Implementation should flow directly from the vision-path. It should be done in accordance with the priorities that have been agreed on by the vision community. The implementation stage will continue for as long as the congregation is still engaged in the change process. The specific actions will change over time, but the church should always be implementing new efforts to continue moving closer to the vision.

Even though implementation is a single stage, it is not a single activity. A helpful way to think about implementation, and its relation to the vision, is shown in Figure 5.1 as a branched diagram. Each level in the diagram—vision, visionpath, and goals and action plans—is more detailed than the prior level. Each is also directly related to the one before. Vision is the broadest and most general level. Visionpath is the next level of detail and generally has several branches from the vision. Goals describe the measurable results that are expected as the congregation follows the visionpath. Action plans are the tasks of implementation. They describe the specific activities that will be undertaken to accomplish the visionpath and goals.

Implementation goes hand in hand with empowerment (Stage 6). Both are long-term, ongoing efforts. They require close coordination. Empowerment should be done in direct support of the agreed-on implementation priorities. The implementation activities, however, tend to be more visible to the congregation and are seen as relating directly to the vision and visionpath. Successful implementation requires the use of

FIGURE 5.1   Relation Among Vision, Visionpath, and Action Plans

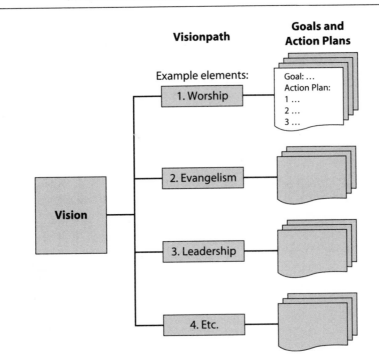

three important skills—systems thinking, planning, and managing—to answer the following questions: (1) What should be done to move toward the vision? (2) How are we going to do it? (3) How can we ensure that we are making progress?

Systems thinking, which is discussed in Chapter Ten, is put to practical use at this stage. Two key terms in our definition of the implementation stage are *coordinated* and *high-leverage.* Systems-thinking skills enable leaders to identify the highest-leverage points for implementation based on a holistic view of the congregation and the vision. It also allows them to diagnose issues that span traditional boundaries and to coordinate their responses. For example, a week-night visitation program is a typical approach for outreach. A systems approach starts by asking whether outreach is a high-leverage priority for realizing the vision. If it is, systems thinking looks far beyond a visitation program to consider the worship experience, small group (assimilation) opportunities, follow-up programs, and other specific needs from the perspective of a newcomer. This should lead to an entire set of coordinated actions targeted toward the goal of more effective outreach that may affect many parts of the organization.

Systems thinking is important because it highlights the different actions that are needed. Effective planning determines the concrete steps that should be taken and the related resource requirements. Without planning, implementation becomes random and ineffective. Planning converts the systems analysis into a specific design. In our outreach example, the congregation's leaders might identify the assimilation of potential members through new small groups as a high-leverage action. The planning process should identify requirements such as group leaders, training, meeting space, and child care. It should also consider long-range issues; for example, if this is a new-member class, how will the assimilation process be continued after six months?

In the change process, planning needs to be done at a broader level than individual programs or ministries. Planning at the congregational level needs to foster coordination between action plans and recognize resource limitations. The congregation that attempts to do too much will run short of energy, money, or leadership. Planning should also address the alignment between existing congregational programs and the vision, which is discussed further in Stage 8.

Once the plans are put in place, good follow-through is needed. This is the skill of managing. Too many churches plan a new program and then assume that everything else will happen automatically. Implementation needs to be done with unparalleled excellence. Managing an important action plan is not something that should be left to chance. It requires commitment, passion, and a clear understanding of the vision. It requires people who are willing to "sweat the details" because they know that doing the little things right makes a difference. And it requires people who have a clear understanding of the desired outcome who will continue to drive toward this goal.

Suggested Actions to Foster Change

What must be done to make the implementation effort successful? What is the difference between a change process that results in radical transformation and one that loses steam and becomes "just another program" at this stage? If implementation is not driven out of the direction and priorities of the vision, it is unlikely to succeed. Even though the specific initiatives are different for every congregation, a set of common actions and principles shapes the implementation of those that are most effective.

Be Clear About Priorities

Vision is a description of God's preferred future for the congregation in three to five years. It is not possible to initiate all the changes to accomplish this vision in one round of implementation. This makes it necessary to thoughtfully and intentionally set implementation priorities. One of the *Seven Habits of Highly Successful People,* according to Steven Covey, is "putting first things first" (1989). This is a practice of allowing our long-term objectives (vision) to guide our short-term actions (implementation). It also involves the discipline of staying on course by avoiding unimportant diversions.

At this stage in the change process, the vision should be clear. If the vision community has not determined the highest priority aspects of the visionpath, they should do so immediately. Priorities may reflect a number of factors such as sequencing of events, likelihood of acceptance or achievement, visibility, and resource constraints. Launching a new children's program may be a priority because it will lead to a momentum-building quick success in the early stages of the change process. Leadership training may be a high priority because many subsequent action plans depend on the church having enough people who are qualified to run them. Contemporary worship may not be an immediate priority because it would consume all of the available financial and leadership resources. Implementation should always be driven from a clear sense of priorities.

Plan Before Acting

Implementation should start with planning, and planning should always involve the people who will be responsible for the resulting action plans. The vision community might be involved directly in the planning, in coordination between plans, or in resource allocation.

In planning, one priority from the visionpath is converted into a set of actions. Visionary leaders often struggle with implementation. Their response is, "I don't worry about the details," or "It should be obvious to everyone where we need to go." Plans should be specific enough that someone else can understand and follow them. Action plans should answer three questions: (1) What will be done? (2) When will it be accomplished? (3) Who will be responsible? A clear vision can be undermined by a fuzzy plan.

For example, the summary of a plan for improved Bible study might say, "In order to improve our Bible study, we will conduct monthly training for all small group leaders beginning in October (focused on Bible knowledge and group dynamics); begin two new classes by January 1, one for new members and one for empty nesters; and conduct a church-wide evaluation of the Bible study program every six months, beginning in March." The person or group responsible for each item should also be identified.

Treat Each New Initiative as an Experiment

In some cases, we approach implementation with such perfectionism that we become overly fearful of failing. Congregations agonize over the specific initiatives, as though extra time will help them foresee the future and develop a perfect plan. It is better to develop a reasonable plan, try it, evaluate the results, and then make modifications as necessary. In the Bible study example above, leaders could conduct the initial session and then ask for feedback, as opposed to trying to design a complete program from the outset.

The concept of an experiment or pilot project is extremely powerful at this stage. People are less resistant to a short-term experiment than they are to a "permanent" change. Consider the difference between two statements:

> We're going to add an 8:00 A.M. contemporary worship because we believe it will help us to achieve our vision. This is an experiment, which we will reevaluate in three months.

> The Vision Community and the Elders have decided that our congregation must add an 8:00 A.M. contemporary worship service, which will begin in two weeks.

The simple way that a change is presented can have a great deal to do with its acceptance. An experiment signals that the leaders do not claim to have all the answers. Experiments give people more room to innovate, learn, and improve with less risk of repercussion.

Measure, Measure, Measure

Before beginning an experiment, a scientist defines the desired results and establishes procedures to measure the outcome. Measurement of implementation requires clarity about the goal and processes for evaluating progress. For example, total worship attendance is not an adequate way to measure the effectiveness of community outreach. Instead, the number of visitors in the service or the number of new believers from the community might be tracked. What does a flat attendance trend tell? It may indicate lack of evangelism, but it may also be evidence that many previously faithful members are dropping out—leaving through the back door, as it were. It may even be the result of members being equipped and sent out as ministers. Without adequate measurement, it is impossible to tell.

Change leaders need to help their congregations define and measure the things that relate most closely to the vision. Several different measures are usually needed, corresponding to different goals of the vision-path. Once the measure is defined, it takes time to begin gathering information. In many cases, it will be necessary to refine the collection of information or the measurement itself over time.

A church that refuses to measure progress will not have a clear picture of how it is doing and will have difficulty knowing when its action plans need to change. Without this feedback, it is nearly impossible to lead change. Furthermore, the discussion of how to measure progress toward the vision can actually be a vision-clarifying experience.

Align Gifts with Needs

God knows his vision for a congregation, and he "gifts" a church with a unique mix of individuals in accordance with this vision. Regardless of the urgency to develop specific plans and get started, change leaders need to take the time to match responsibilities with the spiritual gifts, interests, skills, and experience of members. This may be relatively easy to do within the vision community, since members will be aware each other's gifts. As the change process expands and other members are needed to lead new initiatives, it may take longer. The risk of using any "warm body" is not that the effort will be less than perfect but the real possibility of restarting the action plan after a costly delay. God will call out the leaders that are needed to move toward his vision. The best approach is to wait prayerfully until the right person emerges.

Support the Individuals Who Are Responsible for New Initiatives

The early stages of implementation are difficult for those who are on the front line of the change process. Change leaders need to feel supported as action plans are implemented. These individuals are likely to encounter resistance, uncertainty, and cynicism. They will suffer from being pioneers and from being in a fishbowl—there is no template for what to do, but everyone is looking on in great anticipation.

Support can take many forms. The pastor can go to lunch to listen to how the process is going or to discuss the agenda for an upcoming meeting. The vision community leader can tell the congregation that she has utmost confidence in the person who is executing the plan. A feeling of support, without undue pressure or meddling, is a huge boost to the confidence of the individual. This can make a major difference in the quality and pace of the specific implementation.

The Benefits of Implementing the Vision

Congregational leaders generally do not have to be convinced of the benefits of implementation. But they often need to understand the difference between "doing for the sake of doing" and strategically developing and following an implementation plan that is based on the vision. The latter sounds like more work and an unnecessary level of detail, but the benefits include

- Creating better alignment between vision and actions
- Avoiding false starts, which can deal a major setback to the change process
- Efficiently allocating scarce resources
- Linking actions with the vision for all to see

Key Challenge in Implementing the Vision

Coordinating multiple, concurrent action plans and achieving the right pace for the process—in consideration of resource limitations, congregational attitudes, and urgency.

The process of planning for and enacting specific, high-leverage action plans will be repeated many times during the change process. For all of the reasons already described, a limited number of new activities can be sustained at any one time. The image of implementation occurring in rounds is helpful for many churches. As one round of action plans is brought to completion, a new round needs to begin. Of course, it is never this clean. Some action plans require months of work and others only a few weeks. At times, managing one or two new emphases may stretch the congregation to the limit. Change leaders should regularly ask whether it is time to begin new initiatives. In doing so, they need to strike the right balance between pushing too hard and not pushing enough.

We also acknowledge that a structured planning approach, as described in this section, simply does not fit the personality of some leaders or congregations. They have experienced positive results with a more spontaneous approach. This tension between order and chaos is discussed in Chapter Six. Regardless of their style, change leaders need to move from implementation to the creation of long-term momentum and alignment with God's vision.

Stage 8: Reinforcing Momentum Through Alignment

As much progress as the congregation has made to this point, the transformation is still very fragile. *Alignment* is evident when the majority of the people, ministries, and structures of the church are functioning out of a clear understanding and commitment to the vision. As alignment occurs, the change process spreads beyond a few high-leverage action plans. A tangible sense of excitement, expectation, and everyone "rowing in one direction" will permeate the congregation.

In fact, the final stage of the change process is really not the end. As long as God calls us to transformation and our world changes rapidly, congregations will have to change continually as well. So the eighth stage is not a conclusion to the change process but an ongoing effort to adjust to the call of God's vision and to the changes in the world around us.

The need for continuous change goes against the grain of the organizational culture. Those congregations that willingly or even enthusiastically enter into the transformation process inevitably ask, "How long will this process last?" or "When will things get back to normal?" It can be discouraging to learn that a state of ongoing change needs to become the norm. But the evidence is clear and compelling. Barna observes that "our culture completely reinvents itself every three to five years," (1998, p. 8), and he concludes that our churches must be prepared to engage change at the same pace.

The good news is that the most difficult changes may well be those required in the beginning years of transformation. From physics, we learn that a body at rest stays at rest unless an outside force acts on it.

Keeping it in motion or changing its direction still requires energy, but much less that at first. The physics term is *conservation of momentum.* The final stage of the change process is about creating lasting momentum for ongoing transformation.

Having gone through the effort to get this far, why would a congregation's leaders allow momentum to die? Change leaders never want to feel like their efforts have been wasted. But they do face several momentum killers. Many will view the transformation process as a program. This implies that it should have a well-defined beginning and ending.

Fatigue is another momentum killer. It is understandable that change leaders feel burned out and want to scale back on their involvement after one or two years. Many will have added their change responsibilities on top of other duties. Their response is, "Look at how much I've invested and how much we've accomplished—surely we can take a break." They do need opportunities to rest, and the vision community's role will need to be redefined, but this does not mean that transformation should stop.

One factor that contributes to fatigue is the failure to publicly celebrate the successes of the journey. The deep commitment of change leaders and the congregation's progress toward the vision need to be recognized. This simple act can reenergize the leaders and the congregation.

Another momentum killer is when resistance surfaces or resurfaces. In the early stages, it may be possible to avoid some confrontations. To create long-lasting momentum and continue the transformation, the remaining obstacles will have to be addressed. Keeping a traditional staff organization or overlooking nonstrategic expenditures may be possible for the first year or two, but these carryovers of the old structure will eventually need to be brought in line with the vision.

Even without direct resistance, momentum can be crippled if the congregation does not have a growing number of members who are committed to the vision and who are directly involved in its enactment. It is possible to reach Stage 8 through a combination of charismatic personality and the extraordinary efforts of a handful of people. As the process continues forward it must become a congregation-wide effort. Many of the first-round implementation initiatives will require ongoing management, and another round of change efforts will need to be launched.

All of these factors point to the ultimate objective of Stage 8: the alignment of the congregation with the vision. Alignment occurs when all aspects of congregational life are consistent with and supportive of the vision. The vision statement, the implementation plans, and the words and actions of the vision community should clearly point toward the vision. But this is not enough. Alignment means that worship, small group activities, ministries and programs, budgets, decision making, organization, and attitudes of individual members all reflect the vision. Perfect alignment is never achieved. But the more aligned that the church becomes, the more effectively and quickly it will move toward God's vision.

Cal Jennings had been a member of St. Luke's for twenty-nine years and had become the unofficial spokesperson for the congregation's senior adult population during the course of the last fifteen months. There was no doubt in anyone's mind that his contributions had been immeasurable. When St. Luke's first embarked on the change process, Cal had helped many of the newer and younger members of the vision community understand the congregation's rich heritage. As they began to have a clear sense of God's unique call for their congregation, all eyes turned to Cal. Would the church's long-term members be able to support such sweeping changes? Cal's calm but firm assurance that they had to follow God's leading had been a major milestone in the journey. When the time came to present the vision statement and visionpath to the congregation, Cal shouldered a heavy load as he patiently and lovingly met with many of the older members. The large turnout for the final vote and the overwhelming approval of the congregation's new direction were largely due to the commitment to the vision that Cal had helped to generate.

Nearly a year later, Cal asked to meet with Pastor Les Richardson. After reaffirming his commitment to the vision, Cal shared his concern. "The *whole* church voted on the vision, but the action plans that we have launched don't seem to have an impact on all of the members. I can't see that the senior adult ministry is really going to do anything different next month, since it wasn't a priority for our current round of implementation. I can't get it out of my mind that the vision applies to us—the seniors—as well, and that it should make a difference in our ministry."

This led to a discussion about what it means for a congregation to be in alignment with the vision. Over the next several months, the entire vision community became involved in this conversation. Their commitment to the previous action plans did not waver. But they came to see the need for alignment, and they asked Cal and two other vision community members to lead this effort. As Cal met with many of the different groups in the congregation—the senior adults, Bible study leadership, deacons, personnel committee—he always began with the vision. And he always posed the question "What do you and your organization need to do differently tomorrow to help St. Luke's to move toward God's vision."

When Les and Cal met several months later, the pastor remarked, "I guess no church is ever fully aligned with God's vision. And I know that some of our ministries still don't really understand what the vision has to do with them. But the efforts that you and others have made are beginning to pay off. It really is beginning to feel that the church, not just the vision community, is seeking to follow God's vision."

Suggested Actions to Foster Change

Ultimately, momentum for ongoing transformation is a function of two factors: the organization's ability to continually assess current reality, and its ability to create internal alignment around the vision. This stage addresses the questions of how this can be done.

Recast the Vision

The vision should never be allowed to grow stale or be forgotten. Far too often, visions are treated as though they were novels. All of the effort goes into the conception and writing, after which it is put into print for anyone who is interested to read. A church's vision and visionpath should be treated as a living document. Even if God's direction is unchanged, a congregation's understanding of his vision will become clearer over time. God will continue to challenge the church toward a more distant horizon, one that is consistent with the earlier vision but that reveals his plan in greater detail.

Recasting the vision is best done through periodic assessments with the vision community. They should address whether the vision needs to be revised in order to be consistent with their understanding of God's calling. This can be done annually, in a retreat setting or in a series of meetings. The questions for clarification of the vision in Stage 4 can be helpful at this juncture as well. Vision reassessment is also an opportunity to evaluate and plan for communication of the vision. Periodic vision discernment should remind the congregation that following God's path is a never-ending process.

Take Time to Celebrate Wins

Once the gap between current reality and God's vision becomes apparent, the congregation's leaders will feel an unrelenting sense of urgency that drives them forward in the process. The change journey is long and difficult, and one essential step is to pause and celebrate the victories along the way. Celebrating wins is one way to show appreciation to the vision community and other change leaders who have made extraordinary contributions. It is a powerful way to communicate the vision to the congregation and to remind them of the ultimate destination. Celebration is not just about people—it is an opportunity to recognize God's provision and his hand in the process.

Public recognition should be an intentional part of the transformation process. Celebrations should be directly linked to the objectives that were set as part of the vision and visionpath. These milestones should not be too far apart. Kotter suggests that momentum for the change process is best preserved if celebrations occur no more than eighteen months apart (1996, p. 122). These events can take many different forms—as part of a worship service, at a separate ceremony, in a leadership team meeting, in a special article in the church's newsletter. Making them public, regular, and relevant to the vision is the essential factor.

Identify and Implement New High-Leverage Action Plans

At the beginning of Stage 7, the implementation process was limited to a few, high-leverage action plans. All congregations have resource constraints that cause them to defer other possible actions until later in the process. The ongoing transformation process should include periodic reviews to establish new priorities and implementation plans. The congregation that has launched leadership development and spiritual maturity initiatives may be ready to place these newly trained leaders into one or more new efforts twelve months later. The principle of high leverage should continue to guide the selection of specific action plans to be undertaken.

Align Existing Ministries with the Vision

Up to this point, many ministries in the congregation may have gone about "business as usual." The specific initiatives (from Stage 7) and changes in procedures and structures (from Stage 6) may not affect some of the church's weekly routine. In Stage 8, the existing ministries of the church need to be brought increasingly into alignment with the vision. The clearest evidence of alignment is when the leaders of a program initiate their own changes as a result of their understanding of the vision. The youth program may not have been the focus of any implementation initiatives, but its leaders decide to hold several "come-and-see" events for the unchurched. Bible study leaders may decide to teach a spiritual maturity series to better equip their members.

In some cases, leaders of the various ministries will "catch" the vision and begin to take their own steps to create alignment. This should be encouraged. In most congregations, creating alignment requires proactive efforts by the vision community and staff. Meetings with the leaders in a specific ministry can be used to explore how the vision might be applied in their area of responsibility. Each ministry should be encouraged to specify changes that need to be made and to adopt concrete goals. The staff or a vision community member can facilitate this process, offer training where needed, or meet periodically with the ministry leaders to discuss results.

If alignment could be quantified on a ten-point scale, a congregation in transformation would have programs and ministries at all points on the continuum. Creating alignment is not a onetime event. The staff and vision community must recognize this dynamic, and focus on steadily increasing the congruence of vision and actions.

Establish Internal Monitoring Posts

Momentum and alignment occur when there is widespread understanding of and commitment to the vision. The idea of *monitoring posts* is to assess the degree of understanding, commitment, and alignment that has occurred. The vision community should be encouraged to keep their ears open and to proactively make their own assessments of the congregation's momentum. Publishing the vision community membership may encourage others to seek them out with questions or concerns.

Meetings of the vision community should include a time to discuss and resolve any significant issues. If several members report hearing, "This church just doesn't seem to care about the people who built it," some intervention and care is needed in the senior adult segment. If they are hearing, "We seem to be serious about having an impact on our community," the vision community can be more confident that an important message is being heard.

Address Specific Pockets of Resistance

Another physics principle is that "for every action there is an equal and opposite reaction." Resistance is the "opposite reaction" to change. It may not be as scientific as Newtonian physics, but it will occur. Resistance can come in many different forms—confrontational or passive-aggressive, from known troublemakers or loyal supporters, as a result of a specific change or of an incorrect perception. When, where, and how challenges will surface is somewhat unpredictable.

Some loss of members is likely throughout the change process. Even at this late stage, some people will decide that they are not on board with the vision and that they need to leave. When this happens, leaders must be willing to allow people to find a different place to worship and serve. The worst mistake is to compromise the vision to try to retain a few members.

Change leaders must also be prepared to deal with members who choose to "stay and fight." When the resistance is overt and destructive, failure to act on the problem is far worse than the cure. The Bible gives clear principles in Matthew 18 for how to handle these conflicts. If the confrontation is less explicit, sensitive compromise may be warranted. The nature of conflict, particularly in a church setting, requires that congregational leaders use everything at their disposal—prayer, an attitude of humility, frequent outside counsel, their own judgment—in determining how to act. The church in change cannot and should not always avoid conflict. It needs to use wisdom when confrontation arises.

Create an Eye on the Community

No congregation that has made it this far in the transformation process should make the mistake of losing sight of its external environment. Even as specific action plans are being implemented, the vision community should create ways to gather new information from outside the congregation. In a state of rapid and continuous change, this is the only way for the church to be a relevant, shaping force in its community.

Specific activities might include periodic interviews with key external constituencies (such as school principals and elected officials) and with new and departing members. These interviews should ask questions about trends and needs in the community, perceptions of the church, and specific ministry opportunities. Neighborhood surveys and subscription to newsletters or magazines can provide more quantitative demographic information. In all of these, the question to answer is "What trends are emerging in our target community that we need to be prepared to address?"

Define the Ongoing Role of the Vision Community

After the vision has been adopted and an initial round of implementation has been launched, what is the role of the vision community? It is important at this stage that an explicit and formal decision be made to define their ongoing role. Unless the vision community is disbanding, this is also the time to decide when and how to rotate membership in the group. Rotation gives the original members a break, and it creates a larger body that is deeply invested in the vision.

Several alternative ongoing roles for vision communities are shown in Figure 5.2. It is rarely advisable for the vision community to disband. Too much has been invested and too much is at stake for their voice to go silent. The other extreme, with the vision community playing an overall governance role, is usually impractical. Most congregations already have a well-established form of governance and oversight.

The vision community can play a very significant role, however, as the *champion of the vision*. In this case, the vision community's primary role is to discern and communicate the vision and to monitor progress toward the vision. When they believe that the congregation is straying from the vision or is not making sufficient progress, it is the vision community's responsibility to raise this concern. This role, when successfully fulfilled, should lead to increased alignment between existing ministries and the vision.

A more active role is that of *change agent*. This role extends beyond the responsibilities of the champion of the vision. It involves initiating new programs, ministries, procedures, and other changes that may fall outside the existing organization. For example, a church with a traditional Sunday school organization may not have a mechanism to create

FIGURE 5.2   Possible Roles of the Vision Community in Ongoing Transformation

Role	Description	
Disband	Vision community disbands—typically after approval of vision or initial implementation	*None*
Champion of the vision	Vision community focuses on discerning and communicating the vision, challenging the congregation to make continued progress	
Change agent	Vision community goes beyond discerning vision; continues to initiate high-leverage actions	
Governance	Vision community maintains the vision in serving as congregation's primary governing body	*High*

Time Required / Influence on Transformation

nontraditional small group opportunities. If this is an important component of the visionpath, the vision community may need to take responsibility for launching and overseeing the initiative. As the change agent, the vision community does not stop with asking, "Are we making progress?" Instead they ask, "What is the next initiative that needs to be launched?"

Never Stop

The change process never truly ends. The amount of energy that must be poured into the process may be less and the urgency level may decline after its initial peak, but a congregation that decides to rest on its laurels is taking the first step toward decline. This does not mean that the congregation can never pause and catch its breath—we have already noted the importance of celebrating wins. An unrelenting drive toward urgency and change will burn out even the most resilient congregation.

In a marathon, even an Olympic-caliber runner gets refreshments during the race. She may actually slow the pace for brief periods to recharge her body. But if she is not prepared to accelerate again when a competitor tries to break away, her chance of winning is slim. The art of leadership is knowing when to pause and when to press forward. Continually asking whether the vision is still right, determining whether reasonable progress is being made, and making sure that the process does restart after the pauses are high-leverage leadership challenges.

The Benefits of Reinforcing Momentum Through Alignment

The essential benefit of the "final" stage can be summed up quite simply: Failure to establish momentum and alignment will stop the process short of true, deep transformation. It is easy to be lulled into a premature feeling of victory after the first round of implementation. Establishing momentum and alignment will

- Spread the vision from a few strategic initiatives to a congregation-wide effort
- Steadily break down the residual places of resistance
- Instill a new approach for vision-guided, strategic decision making throughout the congregation
- Create the mindset and systems that will help the church stay in touch with its environment and maintain or increase its impact on its community

Key Challenge in Reinforcing Momentum Through Alignment

Creating an environment in which widespread commitment to follow God's vision routinely overshadows fears of continuous change.

There is no "next stage," but the change process is never-ending. The eight stages of the change process need to be revisited often. This cycle becomes a part of the congregation's culture and way of life. So what questions should change leaders ask periodically as they continue in their effort to transform the congregation?

- Is the vision still clear and consistent with God's direction for the congregation?
- Based on our understanding of the vision, are we making adequate progress?
- Are the congregation's different ministries increasingly aligned with the vision?
- What is the next set of priorities that will keep us moving toward realization of the vision?

Another essential question that the congregational leader should be asking throughout the change process is "What new skills must I master to lead the journey effectively?" For these, we turn to the final part of the Congregational Transformation Model—the learning disciplines of transformational leadership.

Chapter 6

The Disciplines of Transformational Leadership

THE NATURE OF leadership that is required to initiate and guide transformation represents a major shift for many congregations. The leadership skills that most pastors have been taught or have "caught" are generally inadequate for this challenge. Although this sounds discouraging, our experience at UBA has shown that the knowledge and skills displayed by the most faithful and effective change leaders can be learned. As the Congregational Transformation Model continued to evolve, identifying and teaching these skills became a priority.

Some leaders are very capable of strengthening the spiritual and relational vitality of a congregation. They are deep spiritual figures with excellent relational skills. Their ability to discern and follow God's will is superb. Other leaders are especially able to help a congregation accomplish specific goals. They are results-oriented and have strong organizational aptitudes. Their ability to move a church from point A to point B is admirable.

While these are important, an additional set of skills is required to initiate and sustain transformation. The need for these skills grows out of the turbulent nature of our culture and the current state of Christianity in America. Church leaders of the past could be successful by gradually improving on what their predecessors had done. In today's context, leaders cannot depend on tradition for many insights. The current setting for ministry demands continuous learning. Entire congregations must develop the capacity to adjust their way of life by learning new competencies. Leaders play a critical role in acquiring these new skills.

Most clergy actually receive little or no formal training in leadership as portrayed in this book. In fact, most seminaries seem to assume a managerial role for the pastor. Beyond preaching, teaching, and pastoral care, they depict leadership primarily as planning and implementing programs and events.

The demand for change and continuous learning is stressful for leaders, especially those who crave security, independence, and certainty and seek to avoid risk, interdependence, and ambiguity. Change leaders will increasingly need to embrace personal challenges, revolutionary paradigms, team learning, and complexity. These correspond to the four learning disciplines of the Congregational Transformation Model.

Transactional and Transformational Leadership

An insightful way of evaluating leadership based on the exhaustive work of James MacGregor Burns (1978) has been developed by many others (Bass, 1985; Lewis, 1996; Tichy and Devanna, 1986). This work distinguishes transactional leadership from transformational leadership.

Transactional leadership is based on transactions or exchanges between leaders and their followers. The followers express a variety of basic self-interests like physical and emotional security. Leaders shape situations in which the followers accomplish the actions desired by the leaders in exchange for rewards that meet the followers' needs. The transactions might include money for jobs, flattery for loyalty, or votes for favors once in office. Transactional leaders tend to set up rules and standards to check for noncompliance and to maintain the status quo. These leaders rely on reactive tactics as they focus on power and politics.

Transformational leadership is consistent with the model used in this book. The transformational leader helps followers embrace a vision of a preferred future. Leaders inspire and empower followers to achieve new levels of personal and corporate performance. They encourage individuals and support innovative ventures. Followers gladly commit to a future they help to create. Because transformational leaders are trusted and respected, followers tend to internalize the spirit and goals of the organization.

When congregational leaders do not exhibit transformational traits, initiating and guiding transformation is very difficult. The transactional mode is much less effective when deep change is required. An important part of UBA's mission has been to support transformational attitudes and disciplines through the Young Leaders program and other training events and consultations (see Chapter One).

The four learning disciplines cultivated by transformational leaders are described in the following chapters. Peter Senge (1990) articulated the disciplines in a business context, but we found ample evidence that they were also being mastered by effective congregational leaders. (Readers familiar with Senge will note that we have not included *shared vision* as a separate discipline. It is incorporated in the other disciplines and in the change process.)

Leadership Paradoxes

In the process of learning from congregational leaders, we discovered that they also had an astonishing ability to blend seemingly incompatible characteristics. We learned from Collins and Porras (1994) that such balance is actually typical of highly successful organizations. These organizations avoid the "tyranny of the or" when dealing with various dilemmas that appear to be mutually exclusive. They choose both quality *and* quantity. They preserve core values *and* stimulate progress. Four paradoxes of effective congregational leadership are described in the remainder of this chapter.

Service and Risk

Faithful leaders, by definition, exhibit a deep spiritual vitality in their relationship to God. Their discipleship consistently shapes every aspect of their lives, including their relationships. Consequently, their relational vitality is also high. One pastor meets a group of members for prayer at 6:00 A.M. every weekday. The pastor's care for his people is powerful and obvious. When the congregation is together, a genuine spirit of support permeates the group. Even in large congregations, transformational pastors have deep relationships with a number of people, thus providing a model for others to follow. The value of service and the practice of servanthood are fostered by everything these leaders say and do.

Does this mean that their leadership style is laissez faire? Do they simply go with the flow of congregational life? Not at all. These faithful leaders simultaneously take risks. They challenge old ways of doing things and initiate innovative actions consistent with the vision. Sometimes these ventures fail, but the leaders learn from experience and move ahead with more wisdom and sensitivity.

Continuity and Change

A transformational pastor of an older suburban church said, "I wanted my people to see that our actions continued the same tradition of dynamic ministry that was important to them, even though we were expressing it in new forms." It is true that many congregations today need to experience radical, discontinuous change rather than incremental course corrections. Effective leaders help church members connect new ministry approaches with well-regarded aspects of the congregation's heritage. They preserve the core values and beliefs of the congregation.

At the same time, few actions are more demonstrative of a transformational leader than the discernment of a fresh and inspirational vision of the future. The leader's spiritual depth means that the new direction come from God, and the leader's passion for the dream motivates the entire congregation to begin implementing the exciting new direction God has given them.

Team Learning and Personal Accountability

By disposition or experience, many church leaders are inclined to use a "lone ranger" style of leadership. They tend to interact with other leaders only as necessary. But leaders who generate effective change create strong teams, even when it is their natural preference to work alone. They learn how to function interdependently with others. In so doing, they are able to achieve far more than the combined efforts of a group of individuals (see Chapter Nine).

However, faithful leaders do not hide in teams or become inappropriately dependent on others. Rather than attempt to shield themselves, these leaders demonstrate remarkable levels of personal accountability. They say to their members, "This is what I'm doing about our shared commitments." Their personal credibility increases as a result. So does their capacity to model, with great integrity, the attitudes and actions they desire from team members and the congregation.

Order and Chaos

Church transformation requires that all three dimensions of the model flourish—vitality, process, and disciplines. This requires dealing with both planning and flexibility, with both order and chaos. Of course, some leaders may prefer the predictability of order, and others are more comfortable in the spontaneity of chaos. Henry Mintzberg's description (1994) of how organizational strategies evolve is informative at this point. He notes that some organizations (and leaders) prefer to plan their actions carefully and then follow their plan, which results in an actual or "realized" strategy. Other organizations also develop a realized strategy, but they do so by repeatedly acting in certain ways. As a consistent approach emerges over time (rather than having been planned in advance), it becomes their strategy.

For example, one congregation might say, "We should care for the hurting people around us." They form specific plans to achieve their common conviction. Ultimately, the church becomes engaged in a variety of commendable community ministries. Another congregation might not have such an intentional plan, but find themselves responding to the needs of community residents in ways consistent with their values and beliefs. As they continue to respond to these needs, they become equally engaged in community ministries. Neither approach is "wrong." Effective change leaders should recognize their own biases toward order or chaos and should lead their congregations to incorporate the benefits of both.

One prevalent image is that leadership is a natural ability and that anyone who is not a "born leader" will never amount to anything as a leader. We readily acknowledge that some individuals have a powerful natural gift to lead groups. The disciplines and skills that we discuss are perhaps more intuitive to them. Our experience diverges from the conventional wisdom, however, in the implications for those who have to work at leadership. With time and dedicated effort, leadership skills can be learned. Congregational leaders can become more effective by mastering the learning disciplines of transformational leadership—creative tension, mental models, team learning, and systems thinking.

Chapter 7

Discipline One: Generating and Sustaining Creative Tension

WHEN GALEN CALLED, the first words he spoke were, "I need help." Galen pastored a church in another city. At thirty-seven years old, he had recently received his Ph.D. from a denominational seminary and had been in the ministry for more than a decade. "I'm not sure exactly what to ask. I thought I had the right education. I know I can preach and care for people in crisis. But when it comes to getting the whole congregation mobilized to reach the community, I'm clueless."

Where does one begin? Many pastors today struggle with this same question. They have been trained to preach and shepherd a congregation, but few have been exposed to the dynamics of leadership.

The beginning place is the disciplined capacity of leaders and organizations to generate and sustain *creative tension.* Creative tension occurs when a compelling vision of the future and a clear picture of current reality are held in continuous juxtaposition. *Personal mastery* is the shorthand term that Senge (1990) uses for this discipline.

What drives change? Most pastors and church leaders today recognize the need for change. Yet change efforts often stall out and do not produce the intended results. Change is driven when a significant gap exists between a vision of the future that people sincerely desire to achieve and a clear sense that they are not achieving that vision. As this recognition grows, so does their willingness to change their perspective and to try new approaches. This is the point at which they are experiencing creative tension. The discipline to generate and sustain this driving force is indispensable for change leaders.

Our definition has two distinct parts—*generating* and *sustaining* creative tension. Tension is *generated* when the gap between reality and vision is made clear. Without this sharp contrast, tension will not occur. It is the assignment of leaders to generate creative tension—in their own lives and in the life of the congregation. By implication, it is the role of leaders to guide the process of developing and communicating a clear picture of current reality and a clear vision of God's preferred future.

Once tension is generated, it also must be *sustained*. The human spirit moves to reduce the tension caused by a gap between the ideal and the real. Change leaders must keep the tension alive as a force for change. Long-term transformation cannot be accomplished unless the tension is sustained.

Creative tension should be distinguished from crisis or destructive tension. If the tension is too great, a fight-or-flight encounter follows. If the tension is too little, there is no motivation to change. If tension is generated over insignificant issues, the leader's credibility is diminished. Creative tension focuses on the critical issues and is strong enough to motivate change, but not so intense that it becomes destructive. Discerning the level of tension that a group or congregation can live with is an art.

Jesus was the master at generating and sustaining creative tension. He compared the righteousness of the Pharisees (current reality) to the righteousness of the Kingdom (vision) (Matthew 5:20). He compared the culture's image of a leader with his own model of a servant-leader. He challenged their notions of what was most important in life (Luke 12:16–21). And he sustained this tension in the face of opposition on all sides.

Three interactive aspects of generating and sustaining creative tension must be exercised at the personal and the organizational levels. These components are (1) discerning and describing a vision that comes to be broadly shared, (2) communicating a clear picture of current reality, and (3) engaging in the processes that generate and sustain creative tension.

Discerning and Describing a Shared Vision

A shared vision starts with individual visions. The creative spirit is part of the image of God that is in all of us. We are created to dream, to aspire, to become a part of something that is greater than ourselves. Yet far too often in organizational life, the creative spirit has been squeezed out of the individual. Institutional hierarchies are designed for compliance, not innovation.

Congregations that harness the power of the human spirit help individuals clarify their personal vision. Jesus' call to find one's life by giving it away is the clarion call to servanthood that taps the deepest sense of personal vision (Matthew 16:25). Yet even the institutional church can become a place where personal vision is squelched, as resources are harnessed to preserve the institution.

In recent years growing attention has been given to the need to help individuals clarify their personal mission or vision (Blanchard, 1992; Covey, 1989; Maxwell, 1997). While some of this attention has a secular flavor, we believe that God has a unique plan for each of his children. Change leaders who desire to build deep commitment to a shared vision need to begin by clarifying their own personal vision, and helping other individuals in their congregations do the same.

As individual visions become clear, mobilizing groups of people to pursue a shared vision becomes more practical and powerful. Individual members will look at the congregation to decide whether their participation is consistent with their personal vision. Change leaders should be clear about the relationship of personal vision to shared vision. Where personal visions and congregational vision are not aligned, individuals will not be fully committed. It behooves leaders to pay attention to the personal vision of individual members as they seek to build shared vision. (See Chapter Four for an in-depth discussion of the process of discerning a shared vision.)

Commitment Versus Compliance

Senge (1990) distinguishes the possible responses that individuals can have to a vision. These levels of response, summarized here, constitute a helpful framework for assessing the level of commitment in any congregation.

- Commitment: Members (vision community) want the vision and will make it happen. Individually and together they will embrace whatever change must be made to see the vision realized.

- Genuine compliance: Members want the vision but will only make changes that are within the spirit of existing processes and procedures.

- Formal compliance: On the whole, the congregation sees the benefits of the vision. Members do what is expected but nothing more.

- Grudging compliance: Many members do not see the benefits of the vision. But they do not want to risk breaking fellowship with others, especially key change leaders. So they do just enough of what is expected, while making it known that they are not really on board.

- Noncompliance: Most members do not see the benefits of vision and will not do what's expected. "I won't do it, and you can't make me."

- Apathy: Neither for nor against vision. No interest. No energy. "Is it time to go home yet?"

Getting to Commitment

The need for commitment is a central thesis of this book. Congregational transformation will not happen if change leaders settle for compliance. Only when deep commitment to a shared vision emerges can true transformation occur. Change leaders should reflect deeply on the process of gaining commitment to a shared vision. Often their actions inadvertently result in eliciting compliance. Specific ways of building commitment to a shared vision follow.

Clarify Your Personal Vision

As explained above, shared vision grows out of individual visions. The pastor and other key leaders (vision community) should all engage in the discipline of writing a personal vision statement. This is risky because it can lead to an awareness that the visions of the leaders are vastly different. But failure to recognize these differences early in the process can lead to ongoing conflict that saps individual and corporate energy. More often, leaders find a great deal of overlap in the individual visions within the congregation. Clarifying and coalescing these into a larger comprehensive vision is much less efficient than merely allowing the pastor to announce his or her vision. But it is ultimately much more effective because it results in a deeper level of commitment and unity around the corporate vision.

Teach the Congregation About Shared Vision

Jesus spent three years with a vision community of twelve people. He also taught a larger group of followers as often as he could, and he instructed through a variety of media. Vision discernment can be taught in many ways. Change leaders who have successfully gained commitment to a shared vision can be invited to speak to your leaders. Encourage them to be honest about the temptation to settle for compliance and the challenge of getting to commitment.

Encourage the Church to Establish a Vision Community

When the timing is right, this group should be charged with developing a vision statement for the congregation (see Chapter Three). From the beginning, it is critical to establish an environment where diversity is valued and differences of opinion are expected. Each member of the vision community needs to feel cared for and appreciated.

Enlist an Intercessory Prayer Team

A team can be enlisted to pray specifically for the vision community and its ongoing work. Intercessors should ask that God will enable each member of the vision community (1) to be open to other opinions and perspectives, (2) to make a commitment to personal growth, (3) to be willing to engage in positive conflict, and (4) to have the ability to discern God's leadership.

Communicate the Vision

The vision needs to be put in writing, and many different forms of communication should be used to get feedback. Feedback should lead to adjustments that bring increasing clarity and shared meaning to the written vision. (See Chapter Four.)

Continually Monitor the Commitment Level

Healthy congregations have good feedback systems. As change occurs, commitment levels will vary. For some people any change calls for a "withdrawal from the emotional bank account" (Covey, 1989). When the account is overdrawn, people become unwilling to make further changes. As withdrawals are made, change leaders should intentionally replenish the account through acts of kindness, good communication, love, and concern. Commitment will ebb and flow, so effective leaders continually seek to renew it.

Communicating a Clear Picture of Current Reality

Getting commitment to a shared vision is only part of generating and sustaining creative tension. Effective change leaders also help the congregation hold a clear view of current reality. Creative tension is expressed when change leaders hold an uncompromising willingness to discern, acknowledge, declare, and act on the truth.

Cornerstone Church struggled with this aspect of creative tension. For almost twenty years, the congregation had been vibrant and growing. Solidly established in a middle-class neighborhood, the church had effectively reached people for most of its history through standardized denominational programs. In the late 1980s, circumstances changed dramatically. The city's economy weakened, housing values around the church declined, and the entire community began to change. The church's response was to keep doing the things that had worked in the past. For several years, attendance declined gradually. Then from 1990 to 1994, average worship attendance dropped from 420 to 150.

In the early stages of decline, some leaders began to take notice. As they expressed this concern—at first privately and increasingly publicly—Pastor Jesse Williams responded defensively. He felt that he was being blamed for the decline. In some cases he was, but the prevalent sentiments of the congregation's leaders were support for their pastor and a genuine desire for guidance in response to this challenge.

Pastor Williams was reluctant to take a close look at the factors that contributed to the decline. His first response, consistent with his style of handling conflict, was to deal with criticism by attacking his opponents. In this environment, some key leaders left the church, and others remained but were demoralized. As the rate of decline increased, Pastor Williams redoubled his efforts to motivate the congregation to work harder at the things that brought success in former years—and in different circumstances. Ultimately he resigned, battle-weary and defeated. The congregation was left wounded and confused.

What could have been done to prevent this from happening? For the foreseeable future, change leaders will be faced with ongoing, discontinuous change as the norm. Clinging to an image of the world as it once was helps no one. Change leaders must be prepared to discern and acknowledge the truth of their current reality.

Cornerstone had followed a particular model of congregational life that worked for nearly twenty years. Did previous success make them unwilling to examine their methods? Or had successful use of these methods caused them to lose sight of the end result they were seeking to achieve? Was the congregation's decision-making process structured in such a way that the pastor carried too much of the burden for congregational decisions? If so, how did this affect the pastor's response to criticism when it came? These questions and others like them illustrate how difficult it is to get a clear sense of current reality.

Practicing Discernment

Effective change leaders must learn and practice a variety of means for discerning current reality at the personal and corporate levels. At the personal level, self-understanding is an important skill that aids in the discernment of reality.

A leader's self-understanding will influence his or her ability to perceive reality accurately. Every person is broken, marred by sin (Romans 3:23). This brokenness affects how we view the world and prevents us from seeing some things. Unless change leaders have the capacity, in humility, to acknowledge their need for others, their ultimate ability to lead will be limited. God places us in the body of Christ for that very reason. One person sees what another cannot, and together we see reality much more clearly.

The Cornerstone story could have had a very different outcome. When the decline became apparent, the church could have brought together a diverse group of mature Christians. From their divergent points of view, a clear assessment of their status would have emerged. Listening sessions could have been conducted. Surveys that focused on assessing the morale of the members could have been completed. That knowledge could have led to a different and more effective response to the change in their community. Instead, Pastor Williams felt threatened. He attacked those with different ideas, thereby reinforcing his as the only acceptable view of the situation.

The easy road for change leaders is to assume that their views of reality are "correct." Listening to others and allowing yourself to be influenced by their perceptions of the world is risky.

Wise change leaders recognize the complex nature of discerning reality, and they regularly update their picture of that reality. Some of the tools and approaches for doing so are discussed in Chapter Three. But personal mastery involves more than *discerning* reality. It is also about *acknowledging* that reality.

Publicly Acknowledging Reality

Some leaders fear acknowledging reality for fear of being blamed. And indeed this is a risk. Standing before the congregation to say, "Our church is not getting the job done," creates a void that demands action. Many leaders fail in the discipline of creative tension because they are unwilling publicly to share their view of current reality.

As I (Jim) consulted with one congregation, the planning group came to the consensus that the congregation had a dangerously low level of spiritual and relational vitality. The awareness in this poignant moment was painful, but it was clearly shared. The group prayed and set their next meeting with the agenda of addressing this problem.

A few days later, one of the church's leaders called to say that the meeting was canceled and that my services were no longer needed. This group, having discerned current reality, did not have the courage to "go public" with the information. Acknowledging current reality is essential in the discipline of creative tension.

Once change leaders have discerned and publicly acknowledged current reality, a basis has been established for mobilizing people to act. The change process described in Chapters Three through Five provides clear guidance for change leaders in achieving these tasks.

Processes That Sustain Creative Tension

Creative tension is exercised when change leaders paint two pictures clearly. The first picture is of God's vision for the congregation. The second is an accurate depiction of current reality. It is a great challenge, but when change leaders successfully hold both pictures side by side for the congregation to see, they begin to *generate* creative tension. Out of this tension, the energy to drive the change process is produced. It is also through this tension that *generative learning*—defined as learning that increases the organization's capacity to achieve the desired results—occurs.

Human nature moves individuals to reduce creative tension. We can do this by making progress toward the vision, distorting the view of current reality, or compromising the vision. Any of these will relieve the tension, but only the first response leads to transformation. Change efforts fail, in part, because the leaders are unable or unwilling to *sustain* creative tension long enough to allow learning and change to occur.

The Crossroads Church is a five-year-old congregation in a growing suburban neighborhood. It recently completed a multipurpose building that doubles as a gymnasium and a worship center. When the building was completed, Pastor Bruce Robertson announced that a new youth basketball league would begin the following Thursday evening. This was an intentional effort to pursue the congregation's vision of reaching its community for Christ. The program would include a thirty-minute Bible study for youth ages thirteen to eighteen followed by two hours of open gym time. Adult workers would lead the Bible study and supervise the basketball game. On the first night twenty-two teens showed up.

The ministry flourished. Most of the young people who attended were the children of adult church members. One Thursday night, one of the church kids brought a friend. Bruce learned later that this guest was a member of a new but growing youth gang in the community. This young man liked what he experienced at Crossroads, and he came back. Within a couple of weeks more than a dozen of his friends—all members of his gang—were coming.

One Thursday night several weeks later, a fight broke out. A gang member pulled out a knife and threatened a teen from the church. The fight was broken up and Bruce closed the gym for the evening. As soon as he got home, he was besieged with calls from concerned parents. One particularly irate father, Fred Jackson, was Bruce's friend, a church elder, and a strong financial supporter. He expressed his dismay over what had happened and demanded that the pastor "do something to keep that kind of kid out of our church."

In that moment, Bruce faced a dilemma with no apparent solution. He could give in to the demands of this father and friend. In doing so he would diminish the vision of the congregation. He could seek to pacify Fred and the others by declaring that the fight in the gym was not as bad as it seemed. This would distort current reality.

Bruce did neither. Instead, he acknowledged that Fred's concern was legitimate and that the problem was serious. But he also reiterated the call to reach the community, and suggested that the elders meet to discuss the situation, pray, and decide what to do.

Bruce was *sustaining creative tension*. He resisted the temptation to distort reality or diminish the vision. He allowed time for himself and others to work through the situation. Sustaining creative tension also allows the Holy Spirit to work within us. It fuels our prayer life and our capacity for creative thinking. It can make us more open to new ideas. All of that was at work at Crossroads.

The elder meeting generated a significant amount of tension and conflict. Everyone was concerned for the safety of the kids. Bruce courageously guided the conversation, reminding them of the vision that God had given them and asking whether the presence of a gang meant that they should rethink the vision. As the conversation unfolded, the elders seemed to reach an impasse between wanting a safe environment and feeling called to reach their community, including gang members.

After nearly four hours of conversation, the oldest member of the elder team suggested that no decision be made that day. Instead, he suggested that they go to the gym the next Thursday night. He explained, "When Nehemiah was faced with a great challenge, he went out to see the problem first hand. I think there might be some value in that for us." When the elders agreed to this course of action, creative tension was sustained again.

After their Thursday visit, the elders realized how similar these "problem kids" were to their own. God used the experience to soften their hearts. New rules were established to keep the program going while minimizing the risk. Over the next year, four of the young people from the gang were reached for Christ. By successfully sustaining creative tension, Crossroads allowed creative, systemic solutions to emerge.

Effective change leaders recognize that the change process will stagnate without creative tension as a source of drive and energy. The pressure to reduce the tension can be overcome in a variety of ways.

Acknowledge That Tension Is Necessary

Change leaders must acknowledge that tension is a necessary part of the process. In consulting with congregations, we often spend an entire session with the vision community discussing the consequences of change. The concept of creative tension—what it is, how to recognize it, and ways to sustain it—is central to this session.

At a break in one of our seminars, a fifty-five-year-old pastor responded, "My way of thinking has changed today. For most of my ministry, I've assumed that things are going well when everyone is happy. You've helped me see that leading change means in some seasons, not everyone will be happy, and that this may well be a sign that I'm on the right track."

Unhappiness is not an explicit goal of change, and not all unhappiness is a sign that creative tension is at work. Leaders must be discerning. But it is clear that creative tension generates some level of discomfort that drives the change process. Leaders must embrace that reality.

Allow Others to Share the Tension

Change leaders should continue to work on the *community* aspect of vision community. Burdens are lighter when shared. No one likes tension. Most of us, if left on our own, will be tempted to reduce it prematurely. Sharing the pressure of leadership with the vision community is a key strategy for sustaining creative tension. Taking time in each meeting of the vision community to share stresses and concerns will help share the load. Significant times of prayer should characterize the vision community in times when creative tension is high.

Develop Conflict Management Skills

New skills should be developed before conflict emerges. When it does emerge, patiently using these skills can produce new options and alternatives that lead to deeper commitment and better solutions. During conflict is when leaders are most likely to fumble the ball. When conflict arises, most of us revert to patterns learned in our family of origin. For many, these patterns are unhealthy and counterproductive for building shared vision. Conflict management skills should be taught early and reinforced frequently if creative tension is going to be sustained.

Leaders can learn to understand their style of dealing with conflict and to develop the ability to select a style that is appropriate for the situation. In his very helpful booklet *Discover Your Conflict Management Style,* Speed B. Leas (1997) identifies six styles for managing creative tension.

- Persuading—attempting to change another's point of view, way of thinking, feelings, or ideas.

- Compelling—using physical or emotional force, authority, or pressure to oblige or constrain someone to do something that another group or person wants done.

- Avoiding, ignoring, fleeing, accommodating—*avoid* means to evade or stay away; *ignore* is to act as if the conflict is not happening; *flee* means to actively remove yourself from the arena of the conflict; *accommodate* is to go along with the opposition.

- Collaborating—working with those with whom you disagree to find a mutually agreeable solution to a problem. (This is similar to Stephen Covey's principle of win-win solutions.)

- Negotiating—seeking to get as much as you can, assuming that you will not get everything you want.

- Supporting—caring for each person as a child of God.

In his booklet Leas provides an assessment tool that helps individuals determine their one or two preferred conflict management styles. He then describes the circumstances under which each style will be most effective. Recognizing that conflict is likely to occur and being able to choose the most appropriate style to deal with it increases a change leader's chances of success.

Continue to Clarify the Vision

Fuzzy visions are easier to compromise than explicit ones. Fuzzy visions allow for incongruence to exist within the congregation. The outcome can be ongoing, low-level conflict that saps the spiritual and relational vitality of the congregation. An intentional effort to clarify the vision will bring this conflict to the surface. Although this may seem like a setback, clarifying vision will produce significant energy over the long haul that helps the congregation move ahead.

Make Time for Personal Renewal and Reflection

This is perhaps the most important and most counterintuitive strategy for holding creative tension. In the face of tension, our temptation is to do something—anything, even if it is wrong. Change leaders are encouraged to take time to get away as tension emerges. Personal renewal is not synonymous with fleeing. There is a difference between running from conflict and making space to more clearly see what is happening in the midst of the conflict.

The senior elder in the Crossroads story was creating space when he suggested that they defer their decision. After venting their feelings and getting as much information as possible, these elders took some time. Often this is when the Holy Spirit will do the creative work of changing hearts and clarifying thinking. Being intentional about personal spiritual disciplines and about rest can be critical strategies when sustaining creative tension seems impossible.

Many congregations today have been in decline for years but are unwilling to face that hard truth. These churches are fond of saying, "This is a great place. We really love one another." But they are not willing to admit that they are dying a slow death that is robbing the next generation of an opportunity to know the gospel.

Is this truth hard to hear? Yes. But is it accurate? Again, yes. Telling the truth alone, however, is likely to produce only defensiveness and discouragement. The truth about current reality must be placed alongside a clear and compelling vision of the future to which God is calling his people. We serve a God of hope and redemption. He calls us to an exciting future. Generating and sustaining creative tension are part of how he moves in his church.

Conclusion

For a congregation to achieve long-term transformation, all of the disciplines must be mastered. They work in tandem. It is possible to begin learning any one of them independently, but mastering one requires mastery of all. The order for these four chapters on disciplines does not reflect a prioritization or a necessary sequence. Rather, the disciplines are simply listed in the order in which the UBA staff began to recognize and learn them.

For the UBA team, learning to generate and sustain creative tension was the first discipline in which we began to become adept. This unfolded in two distinct phases. Initially we came to grips with the fact that we had been losing ground for forty years (see Chapter One). We simply began to inform our constituents that we were not making progress, despite what had been reported in the past. This clear picture of current reality generated a great deal of tension.

Then we described a vision of healthy congregations. We defined health in terms of disciple-making and community impact, not as increases in attendance in existing programs. This vision, held in contrast to the picture of current reality, generated the creative tension needed for change.

Sustaining that tension was a struggle. Countless forces are at work to maintain the status quo in the face of change, both in judicatories and in individual congregations. In February 1993, I (Jim) was nearly fired. I made some critical mistakes by trying to push the change process too aggressively. A group of pastors who had consistently resisted the new vision took advantage of my mistakes and accused me of wrongdoing in a letter that was sent to every pastor in UBA. This led to a series of meetings to investigate the charges, most of which were proved false. The charges that were accurate were the results of honest mistakes made in the press of the change process. The core leadership of UBA understood this. They chose to forgive me and to reaffirm the vision that God had given us.

Every transformational leader will face these kinds of trials. It would be nice if a passion for God and a desire to serve his people was enough. It is not. Leaders must understand that the discipline of juxtaposing vision and current reality is painful at times. But progress cannot be made without the tension created by this discipline. Generating and sustaining creative tension is the foundational discipline for congregations that seek to discern and follow God's vision.

Chapter 8

Discipline Two: Harnessing the Power of Mental Models

A FRIEND COMES into your office and says, "I've got a headache." You respond, "Take an aspirin." That brief exchange illustrates the power of mental models. Both parties are able to use common terms about the situation and a possible response because of their shared premises. *Mental models* are the images, assumptions, and stories we use to interpret our world and guide our actions. Mental models are synonymous with *paradigms*, a concept thoroughly explored by Thomas Kuhn (1970) and popularized by Joel Barker (1992). Both terms refer to the information and assumptions that shape how we understand and respond to the world around us.

All of us have mental models. Every day, our brains are flooded with information of all kinds. Mental models are a gift from God that enable us to process this information into a smaller, more manageable set of data.

In the above illustration, both individuals hold a mental model about how the human body works. The shared assumptions that form this mental model make it possible to prescribe a course of action without a trip to the doctor for diagnostic tests. Through centuries of research and experimentation, medical science has created a mental model of the human body that is deeply ingrained and widely accepted.

The Power of Mental Models

Mental models help us take very complex dynamics and simplify them in order to deal with them on a routine basis. Mental models are the tools that we use to make leaps of abstraction from millions of individual pieces of data. A *leap of abstraction* occurs when our brain recognizes a pattern or similarity to other experiences based on a very limited amount of information. We quickly draw a conclusion that could not have been reached without the mental model. Rather than analyzing all of the details, we assume that the current situation is like those others, and we respond on that basis. This shortcut for dealing with information is a valuable tool, as long as the leap of abstraction is an accurate one.

If my car suddenly sputters to a stop, my first step will not be to read the owner's manual. I will check the gas and temperature gauges because of my mental model of how a car operates. If the problem is more serious and I simply add a gallon of gas (without checking the gauges), I may damage the engine by trying to restart the car.

Mental models cease to be valuable when the assumptions or generalizations on which they are based are inadequate or no longer correct. A clear biblical example of a mental model is the disciples' beliefs regarding the Messiah. Their assumptions about his long-awaited coming revolved around the political state of Israel. When God anointed earthly kings to rule Israel, they governed the people with political power and the use of force, just like every other nation. When Jesus arrived on the scene, the people of Israel had lived for years in subjugation to other countries. And so they held tenaciously to the hope that the Messiah—an earthly king—would one day come and return Israel to political freedom and prominence.

When Jesus began his public ministry, the disciples believed him to be the Messiah. A few key pieces of data fit, so they imposed on him all of their beliefs and assumptions regarding a political Messiah. They fully expected him to eventually overthrow the Romans and establish an earthly kingdom. Even after his resurrection they came to him and asked, "Lord, are you at this time going to restore the kingdom to Israel?" (Acts 1:6).

Jesus' experience with his disciples is instructive. It demonstrates how powerful mental models are. Jesus taught the disciples on many occasions that he had come to establish a new kind of kingdom. He taught servanthood and a new order, one that was not based on power. But in hearing his message through their ingrained mental models, the disciples completely misunderstood God's plans.

History is full of examples of individuals or groups holding on, even as their existing mental models become inadequate. When Copernicus discovered that the sun, and not the earth, was the center of our solar system, the establishment (including the church) resisted. Nazi

Germany was able quickly to conquer Europe, in part because the French and British were still using a World War I mental model of trench warfare and incremental ground advances. Even many Christians used faulty mental models to defend the practice of slavery well into the nineteenth century.

As the world has transitioned from the industrial age to the information age, we have become more aware of the impact that mental models have on our perceptions of reality. The discipline of mental models requires that we recognize the mental models that we hold, assess them in light of current reality, and have the courage to adjust them when the available data do not fit.

We faced the challenge of mental models as we sought to bring change to UBA. For more than forty years, our pastors and judicatory leaders had defined "doing church" as implementing a set of programs prescribed by the denomination. For many years, this definition was broadly shared and had achieved significant results. As the world around us began to change, we worked harder at what we had been doing rather than challenge our mental models. The results were disappointing and predictable.

Mental Models of the Church

The role of the church in American culture is a key mental model that needs to be examined. The environment in which we serve has shifted dramatically. The church should no longer be seen as a stable institution, but rather as a dynamic organism in a rapidly changing mission field. To appreciate the impact of mental models, consider the assumptions that are made in these two contrasting pictures (see Table 8.1).

In the old paradigm, change occurred incrementally. The church shared the values held by the predominant culture. The pastor was the chaplain-manager of the congregation and was working to reach people who were like the current church members. Most of the programs used by the church were initiated, developed, and marketed by national denominational entities. These programs were standardized so that all congregations within the denomination could use them, regardless of size, local community, or congregational demographics.

In the mission field paradigm, change is rapid and discontinuous. The gap between the values held by the church and those held by the community is clear. The pastor's primary role is leader—one who guides

TABLE 8.1   Two Mental Models of the Church in American Culture

Stable Institution and Context	Rapidly Changing Mission Field
Slow, predictable change	Rapid, discontinuous change
Shared values in church and community	Divergent values in church and community
Pastor as manager	Pastor as leader
Homogeneous target audience	Diverse target audience
Stable strategy developed by denominations	Continuous adjustments made to strategy at local level
Programs developed by national denominational entities	Programs developed by many different organizations
Standardization of approaches	Customization of approaches

the congregation to discern and achieve vision. The vision is usually influenced by the identification of one or more target audiences in the community. As the vision is pursued, the congregation continuously adjusts its strategy without consultation from the national denomination. As specific ministries are developed, the local body will choose resources from a variety of denominational, parachurch, and other organizations.

In one of the congregations where we have consulted, the pastor described the impact of this shift in mental models. "When I went to seminary, the implied message was this: 'If you can preach the Gospel and can effectively manage three or four standard denominational programs, you can have a healthy, growing congregation.' Today that is simply not true. The world in which our congregation ministers is not the same world that my seminary prepared me to shepherd."

He described growing up in a slow-changing, homogeneous community in the Deep South. The church did not worry about strategies because long-term plans and the associated programming were set by the national denomination. The pastor served primarily as a chaplain, and "missions" were viewed as overseas.

His current congregation was in a large, diverse city, and he had learned that mission opportunities were all around. The congregation's approach to disciple-making had changed to the mental model of foreign missionary training. He also described the challenge of developing the necessary leadership skills for this environment—ones that he had not learned at seminary—and the time and effort required for the congregation to shift its mental models. He concluded, "In order to effectively reach my community, I've had to rethink things—a lot of things."

Studies and experience confirm that American society has changed dramatically in the past twenty years. Lyle Schaller (1997) observes that it is "no longer possible to design a program, edit a hymnal, produce a curriculum series, offer a study program, train a youth minister, outline the format for a corporate worship service, fashion a church growth strategy, design a staff configuration, or recommend a system of governance that will meet the needs of every congregation" (p. 13). And yet much of the training that is provided to pastors, the programming in a typical church, the style of worship, and the way that we proclaim our good news is based on beliefs and assumptions that are at least forty years old.

Recognizing and Acting on Mental Models

This chapter does not attempt to catalogue all the changes in our world or to define the most appropriate mental models. Our premise is that mental models exist and that they influence the choices we make. Recognizing the existence and testing the accuracy of the mental models that we use to make congregational decisions is an essential part of transformational leadership. But this is not enough.

Change leaders must also enable their congregations to recognize, embrace, and act on new mental models. Describing of the new models is important, but effective change leaders understand the *implications* of the new mental models and help an organization make the necessary transition. A cluster of skills should be engaged at the personal and the organizational level in order to master this discipline.

Self-Disclosure

The single most powerful personal skill in mastering mental models is the capacity of self-disclosure. Your ability to look deeply within, to understand your strengths and weaknesses, and to know the impact that life experience has on your worldview is a powerful tool.

This kind of self-understanding is essential because our assumptions are based on thousands of personal life experiences. And in turn, our perceptions and actions today are based on the mental models we have developed. For instance, if you were raised in a home where physical abuse was a common practice, that becomes a filter through which you see things. Awareness of how that experience affects your beliefs and assumptions is critical to dealing effectively with mental models. Self-awareness that can be disclosed to others is a key skill in dealing with mental models.

The Gospel of Christ calls us to this kind of authentic transparency. Jesus modeled this self-awareness. He knew who he was (Matthew 3:17). He knew his purpose in life. He knew how his culture influenced him. The apostle Paul tells us not to think more highly of ourselves than we ought—to have sober judgment (Romans 12:3).

Many tools and resources are available today for individuals who want to increase their capacity for self-disclosure. Studying the Bible and its teaching regarding the nature of God, humanity, and the world is one of the best places to begin. The spiritual disciplines of solitude, meditation, and prayer allow the individual to reflect deeply on the issues of identity. Personal profiles that reflect communication style preferences and spiritual gifts are abundantly available. Small groups of many kinds provide a safe setting for individuals to think out loud about themselves. Christian counseling provides a more private means of discovery.

The challenge of mental models may be most significant for Christian pastors. Many have learned in seminary to avoid self-disclosure at all costs. Others have engaged in self-disclosure and had it used against them in unscrupulous ways. Still others enjoy the posture of sitting on a pedestal that far too many church members are willing to encourage.

Individuals who want to master the discipline of mental models begin by committing to a growing sense of self-awareness. This allows them to identify their mental models and test them against reality.

Empathic Listening

When dealing with challenging problems, our perspective is often incomplete. We take our experience with one part of a system and generalize it to the whole. In systems thinking (see Chapter Ten), we learn that dealing with one part of the system gives an inadequate picture of the whole.

The dilemma in overcoming our limited view is that we are often unwilling to learn from others who interact with other parts of the system. Instead, we try to persuade them to adopt our position. Steven Covey (1989) discusses the impact that *empathic listening* can have in problem solving. "Empathic listening is so powerful because it gives you accurate data to work with. Instead of projecting your own autobiography and assuming thoughts, feelings, motives, and interpretation, you're dealing with the reality inside another person's head and heart. You're listening to understand" (p. 241).

Covey also correctly asserts that many people have years of training in reading, writing, and public speaking, but few have training in how to listen. If one cannot listen to the perspective of others—openly, honestly, and without judgment—it will be much more difficult to understand the assumptions and beliefs that others bring to the conversation. When change leaders learn to listen empathically, they learn to see the world differently.

Randy Calhoun is pastor of a church of one hundred forty parishioners in a transitional neighborhood in a midsized city. He and his wife, Lisa, are both thirty-three years old. They have two preschool-age children. Randy's mom and dad divorced when he was eight years old, and his dad was mostly absent from his life afterwards. His mom dated a little as he was growing up, and he developed a brief friendship with an adult man at his church. But after about a year, the man was transferred to a new city. Randy longed for a father in his life.

When he became pastor of the Illinois Avenue Church, one of the attractive things about the congregation was Bill Wooley, the sixty-eight-year-old man who chaired the elder board. Bill had an affable, engaging personality, and he and his wife immediately took Randy's family under their wing. The two families spent a lot of time together at church and in each other's homes. The Wooleys became adopted grandparents to Randy and Lisa's children. Randy remarked to Lisa at the end of their first year at the church, "It's like I have finally found the dad I never had."

As Randy's tenure unfolded, the church began seeking to clarify God's vision for them. Bill was deeply involved in the process. One day, nearly six months into the experience, another elder came to Randy. "I'm concerned that Bill Wooley is having too much influence on this process. It seems that no matter what he suggests, you give in to him."

That conversation triggered a new awareness for Randy. As he honestly listened, he had to admit that there were times when he disagreed with Bill but was afraid to speak up. He talked with Lisa and reflected for a long time on the conversation. Ultimately he recognized what many around him had already seen. Bill Wooley was the father Randy had never had. Many of Randy's decisions were driven by an unsubstantiated and unrecognized fear that Bill would leave if conflict emerged—just as Randy's father had done many years ago.

As Randy began to better understand the impact of his father's abandonment, he was able to articulate a childhood fear that somehow his misbehavior had caused his father to leave. As he explored this, he realized he had made a vow as a child—long since hidden from conscious memory—that if his dad ever returned, he would be the model child. He would never cause his father to leave again by being disobedient or by causing a disagreement.

As Randy examined this deeply held mental model that had been invisible for so long, he could see its influence on his decision making. He was able to challenge the assumptions and beliefs on which his model was based. Over time, Randy began to be more honest with Bill—and Bill did not leave.

Self-awareness leads to an increased capacity for self-disclosure. A third key personal skill, the skill of dialogue, builds on these first two. Dialogue is also essential for team learning and is discussed in depth in the next chapter.

The skills of self-disclosure and empathic listening cannot be developed overnight. The basic concepts and techniques can be learned quickly, but mastery takes time and continuous practice. Truly learning the skills of self-disclosure and empathic listening also requires taking risks in interpersonal relationships. Like the game of golf, you can read books about it all day long, but until you actually swing the club many times, you will never begin to master the game.

At the organizational level, the discipline of mental models is highly interactive with the other disciplines. Living with creative tension—the gap between current reality and God's ideal—should lead us to ask whether the mental models on which we have based our decisions are accurate. Establishing performance standards (discussed in Chapter Nine) motivates us to examine our models. Other organizational capabilities that contribute to the mastery of mental models are critical thinking and transformational planning.

Critical Thinking

Using critical thinking intentionally to challenge the mental models of an organization is a key skill. *Critical thinking* is the process of taking a fresh look at a problem by stripping away the assumptions and constraints that may have been imposed in the past. It requires probing deeper than most groups are comfortable doing. It should be used when the organization is facing a significant challenge that previous efforts have failed to resolve. The potential benefits of critical thinking are new insights into our mental models that can lead to unique solutions.

A group of pastors from one denomination worked together to examine their mental model of congregational life. As a group, they had struggled for many years to have an impact on their community, which had numerous social problems that were rapidly worsening. Attendance at most of the congregations was at a plateau or was declining. Many suffered from serious morale problems.

Forty-four of the pastors engaged a consultant to help them think critically about their mental model of the church. In the initial session, the consultant asked the group to complete the statement "The thing that makes the church work is . . ." She acknowledged that God's work through the Holy Spirit is at the heart of congregational life. "Obviously, some things can only be done by God. But what is it that God expects you to do that most significantly contributes to making the church work?"

The group had fun with the exercise. When they finished the consultant listed their responses on the board. Some said effective preaching. Others said small groups. Still others said financial resources were the critical element. The list was long.

When everyone had finished, the consultant made an interesting observation. "Everything you have listed as a factor that makes the church work is a program in which your church is currently engaged." One of the leading pastors responded. "What would you expect? When we went to seminary, we were taught that if we could preach well and manage the denomination's key programs, the church would thrive." Many others in the room nodded in agreement.

The consultant then asked the group to list facts that would cause them to challenge their assumptions and beliefs. The list included the following:

- I've used these programs for a long time. I know how to implement them. They just don't produce the results they once did.
- My church is using all these programs well. We execute every part of the program diligently. And I'm a fair preacher. But our church has been declining numerically for eight years.

- Many of the programs assume a certain level of knowledge about the Bible that many in my community don't possess.

- Seminary did not prepare me to deal with so much diversity in my community. I always assumed that I would pastor a church in a community where the people looked like me and had similar backgrounds and life experiences.

The list went on. At the conclusion, the consultant asked the group to list factors other than preaching and programs that were affecting their congregation's effectiveness. This list included

- The changing demographics of the community
- The changing values and lifestyles of the community
- A history of conflict that was present in some congregations
- Growing unavailability of women who had historically staffed many programs offered by the church

"What do you do with the data that do not fit your mental model?" asked the consultant.

One pastor responded, "Most days I just ignore them. I don't know what to do about it, and when I think about it, I feel overwhelmed and inadequate."

Another said, "We know the current programs are not working. But we don't know what to do to fix them. So we just keep trying and hope that things improve."

The consultant then began to discuss different mental models of the church. The response of the group was varied. Some had "aha moments" in which much of the data began to make sense. Others were more skeptical, and some were resistant. This was the beginning of a five-year period, during which this group continued exploring their beliefs and assumptions about congregational life. They gradually made adjustments based on new information. They learned new skills to support their new mental models. And they began to see improvements in the health of their churches—slowly at first and more dramatically over time. This group's willingness to openly and honestly explore their mental models—individually and collectively—served as a catalyst for significant breakthrough.

Transformational Planning

Planning should be a central process for facilitating congregational transformation. Unfortunately, many congregations use static or incremental planning processes. These plans are based on a set of assumptions that are rarely changed (and are often not made explicit). In many cases, a limited range of options is considered. Planning may simply involve taking last year's calendar and copying the events onto the next year. This approach actually reflects a mental model of the church that is generally inadequate in today's environment.

Transformational planning is much more difficult to do, because it involves many more "moving parts." Under this approach, leaders recognize that a good plan is based on key assumptions and interdependencies, and that as these change, the plan must change also. This book is based on the assumption that spiritual and relational vitality, the change process, and the learning disciplines are three key interdependencies.

As its name implies, transformational planning is more than an annual exercise to set calendars and budgets. Transformational planning embraces the assumptions of systems thinking and calls the congregation to ongoing, continuous alignment of all the congregational systems in order to achieve the vision. Transformational planning is distinct in a number of respects.

Identify Critical Assumptions

Many congregations plan as though the world is still changing incrementally and predictably. With the rapid pace of change, annual budgets make less and less sense. A six-month forecast is more realistic. Many congregations plan as though their community is homogeneous. Yet in every city across America there is increasing ethnic and generational diversity. What assumptions about the external world and the congregation undergird your planning process?

Identify Key Interdependencies

Effective plans recognize the impact that a change in one area can have on other key dynamics in the congregation. These are called *interdependencies*. Because everything in a congregation is connected to and affects everything else, changes in one part of the system will require adjustments in other parts. Intentionally identifying the key interdependencies increases the effectiveness of planning and can help bring about a high degree of alignment (see Chapter Five).

In addition, as noted above, the interdependence among spiritual and relational vitality, the learning disciplines, and the change process is significant. Like a three-legged stool, failure to attend to any one of these three results in a fallen stool.

Create a Safe Environment

Participants in the process must feel that they have permission to raise questions, challenge assumptions, and explore a variety of options. In transformational planning, there can be no sacred cows. Static planning allows leaders to avoid making tough decisions about ministries that have outlived their purpose.

Develop Alternate Scenarios

Making frequent adjustments based on a changing environment is easier when the group has anticipated future possibilities. Accurately predicting the future is not possible. But it is possible to develop scenarios that describe plausible future developments. A scenario combines "hard data" and possible outcomes for other key uncertainties to paint this future picture. For a given scenario, a planning group can anticipate the most appropriate response and can be better prepared to react in the future.

Ask Questions

Many groups have naturally inquisitive individuals who want to explore how and why things work as they do. A traditional planning process that focuses on control (versus learning) tends to squelch this exploration. Empowering the inquisitive person to serve as a catalyst may take time, but it can raise important "how" and "why" questions that the group needs to consider.

Treat the Plan as a Living Document

In traditional planning models, the plan is the end result. In transformational planning the vision is the end result and the plan is regularly adjusted to ensure that the end result is achieved.

The process of continually making adjustments in order to achieve the congregation's vision is a challenging one. But with a clear vision, clear end results in mind, and a commitment to the truth, congregations can continually clarify their mental models and can make significant strides forward.

An Application of New Mental Models

In 1997, John Hill left his staff position at a traditional denominational church to establish the Refuge Church, a new congregation in the heart of a major city. If he had accepted the mental model of the churched culture, the new group would have looked for land on which to build a building. The building would have been designed for worship services, small group discipleship classes, choir practices, youth group meetings, and other typical church events.

By applying the principles of transformational planning and carefully examining their mental models, a very different result emerged for the Refuge Church. John gathered a core group—a vision community—to consider establishing the new church. Rather than assuming that they knew the answers, the vision community met for many weeks to pray for God's direction.

They also began studying the community that they felt called to reach. From demographic data, they knew that the median age was thirty-one and that community included a great deal of ethnic and socioeconomic diversity in a small geographical area. John and his core group began talking to people in the community about their impressions of church. They discovered that many were open to issues of spirituality but had had previous bad experiences or negative impressions of the institutional church. Few were attending a church.

Over time John and the vision community began to make some key decisions. They concluded that their target community had so many negative impressions of the institutional church they it would be virtually impossible to get them to come to a church building. So they decided to hold all church meetings in homes. This is not unusual for a small congregation in its early years, but Refuge's stated plan was to remain in homes. Some people in the city's Christian community were shocked: "How could you have a church that did not have a church building?" The question reflected a mental model that ties congregational life to building an edifice as the central gathering place for a large congregation.

The house church approach is based on an entirely different mental model. Rather than focusing on a single facility that can accommodate all the members, the group splits into new homes as it grows. This allows the congregation to become very large without ever buying land and building a building. The group's mental model reflected specific realities of their community, such as high property cost and a lack of undeveloped land. They also recognized that a home environment would be more inviting to their target community and would help facilitate deeper relationships.

These relationships were an important piece of another mental model that emerged at Refuge. The typical church makes many assumptions about the religious background and Bible knowledge of its existing and potential members. In Refuge's denomination, this translated into a one-hour small group Bible study on Sunday mornings as the primary time for discipling. As Refuge began to reach people from its target community, they discovered that an hour on Sunday morning was not the right solution. They were reaching people who had no knowledge of the Bible and whose lifestyles were radically different from that of a mature Christian. It was clear that a radically different discipling model would be needed.

So the congregation developed a small group discipling process that began with a three-day retreat for new Christians, followed by a weekly three-hour meeting. The meeting included a teaching time, a meal, and an extensive time for discussion and personal application of the presentation. One-on-one meetings between each new believer and a more mature believer supplemented this time. These meetings gave further assistance to the new believers as they dealt with the challenges of making dramatic life changes.

This description of the congregation's decisions does not even begin to capture the "messy" process that led to this place. All of the members of the core group came from existing congregations. All came with a sense of dissatisfaction that the existing churches were not reaching this community. But the difference between knowing what doesn't work and knowing what should be done is enormous. A hundred conversations, formal meetings, and informal debriefings over coffee shaped these decisions. Conflict emerged frequently and several of the initial core group members eventually returned to their original churches. On many occasions, John and other key leaders became deeply discouraged. Only in hindsight did they fully recognize that they were doing the deep work of challenging the mental models that shaped their entire understanding of what a church is.

The process of challenging mental models is not easy. Even when the idea makes sense, many of our assumptions about church life are sources of comfort, security, and balance in our lives. "The way we have always done things" becomes synonymous with "the right way to do things."

Several factors contributed to the Refuge Church's success in challenging its mental models. In the early stages, the vision community had focused on developing a strong sense of spiritual and relational vitality among its members. This served them well when conflict emerged. John and several key members of the core group were naturally inquisitive. They wondered how and why things worked the way they did. This inquisitiveness led them to explore a variety of options and allowed them to live with ambiguity. A number of times they experimented and failed, but they treated each instance as an important learning opportunity. Throughout this formative period, the group had a clear end result—the transformation of a specific geographical area of the city—that guided its decision making.

This illustration demonstrates how deeply mental models can influence all of our choices. We do not suggest that every church should use this specific mental model, sell its property, and restructure its Bible study program. In fact, one of the major risks with books and seminars on successful churches is that they work in a particular context—a specific mental model that is unlikely to be applicable to others. The purpose of this illustration and this chapter is to challenge each of us to think through the assumptions and beliefs that we bring to the table as we seek to lead change in our congregations.

We were recently asked, "Why, after leading successful congregations for more than thirty years, am I just now hearing about mental models?" Mental models are not new. As noted earlier, Jesus' disciples struggled with mental models. What is new for congregational life is the pace of change and the need to scrutinize our mental models. When the pace of change is slow, the assumptions and beliefs about congregational life that have been worked out over a lifetime can be trusted. As the pace of change accelerates, it becomes increasingly necessary for the congregation to make its assumptions and beliefs explicit and then to test them against the reality of its context.

The church planted in the suburbs in the 1950s found it easy to add youth programming and eventually senior adult ministry as the neighborhood gradually aged. The challenge is much greater when the community goes through rapid transition. Yet in seeking to respond to today's challenges, these congregations often use yesterday's mental models. As congregations master the discipline of mental models, they will reap dual benefits. Significant learning will occur for the team that is involved in the process, and the resulting decisions will have a powerful impact as they become the driving force for the entire congregation.

Chapter 9

Discipline Three: Enabling Team Learning

TEAMS ARE THE talk of the day. A growing body of research indicates that organizations cannot reach demanding performance challenges or significant goals unless they develop high-performance teams. Katzenbach and Smith (1993) define a team as "a small number of people with complementary skills who are committed to a common purpose, performance goals, and approach for which they hold themselves mutually accountable" (p. 45). We define *team learning* as the process of enabling a team to produce results far beyond its combined capabilities as individuals. The apostle Paul describes the church as a body. In using the metaphor of a human body to depict the church, he captures many of the aspects of effective teams (1 Corinthians 12:14–27).

The human body is an incredible creation. After years of training, gymnasts from around the world come together in the Olympics and display agility and strength that are unthinkable to the average human being. As they perform, millions sit spellbound by their grace and beauty. The discipline and coordination of muscles combined with the artistic expression of their routines is extraordinary to behold.

The Nature of Teams

God created the church, with its various parts or gifts, to work together to achieve excellence just as the various parts of the gymnast's body do. Paul declares that though we are many parts, we are one body (1 Corinthians 12). When the early church was in conflict over who was most influential, Paul made it clear that he planted, Apollos watered, and God gave the increase (1 Corinthians 3). Both planting and watering are necessary, and both Paul and Apollos contributed what they did best. Though each individual may represent a different function in the church, it is only when they operate in concert that the body is at its best.

These images communicate deeply about teams. Individuals who work on the same church staff or who are a part of the same vision community should bring a rich diversity of skills, spiritual gifts, life experiences, and worldviews. This diversity needs to be appreciated and used to strengthen the church.

Yet that very diversity, which offers the potential for incredible power, often becomes a disadvantage. Many congregations have chosen not to embrace the challenge of diversity. Instead, they have created cultures in which individualism is valued, power and authority are misused, and mutual submission is viewed as weakness. The thesis of this chapter is that forming teams and teaching them to learn is a key leadership discipline. This discipline is called *team learning.*

A Definition of Learning

Before describing teams any further, it will help to focus on the nature of and need for learning. In the context of change leadership, learning is not ultimately about acquiring new knowledge. In Western culture, learning has been robbed of much of its meaning. Learning is often used as a synonym for reading a book or attending a conference. At the close of the conference, the participant's notebook is deposited on a shelf to gather dust. Even so, the attendee will often say, "I've learned."

For transformational leaders, learning expands a group's capacity to achieve its desired results. New information may help to increase the team's capacity to meet its goals, but this information is a means to a larger end. It is at this point that team learning relates distinctly to the discipline of creative tension. One skill of generating and sustaining creative tension is clarifying vision. As the desired results of this vision are clarified, a team has a basis for assessing its abilities and learning needs.

When the pace of change was slower, individual learning could simply be consolidated to accelerate progress toward an objective. One person would take an assignment and then report his or her findings to the group. As the pace of change and the level of complexity have increased, this approach is no longer adequate. Even when a group of individuals works independently and shares the results of their work, they are often unable to achieve their goals.

Team learning is necessary not because people always prefer working together but because the challenges we face are simply too great for individuals or collections of individuals to achieve them. However, teams are hard work. They are inefficient and require us to function interdependently. They can be full of conflict. And for those who are accustomed to hierarchical leadership, teams mean less control. The use of teams should be based not on whether we like them but on how well they allow us to accomplish the God-sized vision that is set before us.

Learning in Teams

Understanding the definition of a team, believing that a team is necessary, and actually building a high-performance team are three different things. We have been conditioned to think of learning and performance on an individual level. Yet when we see great basketball teams, superb jazz ensembles, and other examples of outstanding teams, we know that we are seeing more than a collection of talented individuals executing their respective parts. We are seeing the fruits of team learning.

If we are to turn individual learning into team learning, our intention must be clear. *Team learning* is "the process of aligning and developing the capacity of a team to create the results its members truly desire" (Senge, 1990, p. 236). It is the process of changing the group's purpose from communicating and coordinating to *learning*. It is about taking individuals—with all of their gifts, experiences, and knowledge—and molding them into a living unit that is capable of producing far more than the sum of its respective parts. It is about creating a high degree of alignment, so that the team's collective energy is focused in a single direction.

Teams Versus Working Groups

In the church we often work in groups—church staffs, committees, task forces—but view our tasks and our learning as individuals. In group meetings, we communicate and coordinate individual work so that no one gets on our turf. This is not a team. It is a working group. The distinction between a team and a working group is complicated by the current fad to refer to every working group as a team.

What is the difference between a team and a working group? Katzenbach and Smith describe a *working group* as one "for which there is no significant incremental performance need or opportunity that would require it to become a team" (1993, p. 91). A significant performance challenge does not automatically turn a working group into a team, but it does create the condition in which a team is needed.

Teams and working groups can be distinguished in two important ways. First, teams have significant, shared performance goals. In a working group, each individual member is responsible for his or her own performance. For instance, in many church staffs, the worship pastor, the youth pastor, and the small groups pastor each have separate sets of goals. They meet regularly to coordinate calendars and to communicate regarding potential conflicts, but they do not have any shared responsibility for results.

In a team, however, a common goal is set. These goals can only be achieved through the mutual, cooperative efforts of the members. For instance, the team's goal might be a 20 percent increase in the number of first-time visitors who come to the church a second time. Each member of the team would have some responsibility for achieving that goal. They would work together to identify the possible reasons that only 5 percent of the visitors currently return. As possibilities and options were identified, each individual would have a specific follow-up assignment. One might conduct a survey and bring the results to the group. Another might read and summarize some material to bring back to the group. Another might identify and interview key leaders in at least three congregations that had a high return rate. Each member does real work outside the team meeting to accomplish their shared goal.

A second distinction between a team and a working group is accountability. In a working group, each individual is responsible to a supervisor. In a team, each individual is responsible to the rest of the team. It is much more challenging to be accountable to a team. It requires a level of risk that many individuals are simply not willing to accept.

So why consider organizing your work in teams? There is one primary reason. Is the performance challenge you face so large that a working group cannot achieve it? In most congregations the answer to this question is "It depends." It depends on the scope of their vision. If the vision of the congregation is simply to make incremental progress, a working group is often all that is needed to get the job done. When a church measures progress by comparing this year to last year, effective working groups may suffice. If the congregation's vision is to make an ever increasing impact in its world, or if the vision calls for a radically different approach to congregational life, the performance challenge requires more than working groups—it requires teams.

At UBA, the journey to become a real team was a significant challenge. We found two prevalent but outdated mental models to be critical hurdles: leadership and dependence. These same images often impede building teams in congregations.

Leadership carries strong connotations in our culture. We think of a leader as the person who sets the direction, mobilizes the organization, and molds the group around his or her will. A general sending the troops into battle, and all the attendant assumptions that accompany this image, is the ultimate leader in this mental model. These very images and assumptions undermine our ability to build teams.

As our association moved toward teams, I (Jim) had a nagging sense that I was abdicating my responsibility as executive director. Nevertheless, we formed a team at the highest level called the Director Team. Each team member had specific assignments, but we worked together on key directional decisions. Our covenant was that I would not make any unilateral directional decisions—these would only be made by consensus. This was a much slower, less efficient process. But it resulted in a deep level of shared commitment and understanding within the team and the entire association.

Dependence carries negative connotations for many people. Our society also has a mental model that leaders and other professionals should know the answers to the challenges that they face. Working as a true team acknowledges and demonstrates that we cannot solve the problems on our own. It requires a level of interdependence and vulnerability with which most of us are uncomfortable. The UBA team found that even with a high level of trust, dependence on someone else to achieve shared goals was challenging. Each of us had spent a lifetime learning to be independent. It took time and commitment to learn new work patterns.

In the end, the results we achieved were significantly greater than what could have accomplished independently. We slipped into old habits on a number of occasions, but our belief in the need for diversity and collaboration and our commitment to a challenging vision kept bringing us back to teams.

The challenge faced by congregations today is enormous. The needs of our society are equally staggering. Our thesis is that congregations must be transformed if they are going to have a significant impact on the world. We must accept the *learning challenge*—not the challenge of merely acquiring more information—to discern how to achieve this impact for Christ. This is the task that demands that we master the discipline of team learning.

Two Keys for Team Learning

What are the keys to mastering team learning? How can we align and develop the capacity of a team to create our desired results? What must happen to change a group's purpose to *learning*?

Commitment to Teams

The first key is to make a personal commitment to teams. This is not a trivial decision. Change leaders should expect resistance to team learning. Some people do not believe that a team will outperform a collection of individuals. Some find the team approach too time-consuming. They see the extra time spent in meetings and in new learning but not the benefits. Others find that the open, transparent environment of a team is too risky. They do not want to expose their thinking. Change leaders should examine their own attitudes and assumptions about teams. Before starting down that path, they should consider their own comfort with the level of interaction and disclosure that is required.

The most difficult and crucial step in team learning is for the potential team members to recognize the deep, subtle resistance that each one brings to working in teams. Recognizing and making this resistance explicit to other team members tends to lessen its grip. It takes time for a group to emerge as a team, and all the concerns and resistance related to teams will resurface during this period.

One minister described a recent breakthrough in understanding his reluctance to commit to teams. "My parents fostered an unhealthy dependence between them and their children. When I left home, I was fiercely determined to win my independence. The battle took its toll on me, but I won. It's occurred to me that I'm so protective of my hard-won independence that I've never really learned how to be interdependent."

He went on to describe school and ministry experiences in which he related well to others but had always avoided mutual submission and dependence. Then he said, "I see the value of teams, but God is going to have to change some things in me before I can be a part of one." His candor was refreshing. By accurately assessing his personal challenges, this pastor had taken an important first step toward team learning.

For teams to form and team learning to emerge in a congregation, each team member needs to look closely in the mirror. We all bring contributions to the team. We also bring baggage that can stand in the way of team learning. Clearly identifying these issues will enhance the group's ability to become a high-performance team.

Commitment to Learning

The second key for leaders who seek to master team learning is their resolve to developing the necessary skills (discussed in the next section). Change leaders should assess the skills of each team member and try to create targeted learning experiences at every stage of the change process.

Learning experiences must focus on more than transferring information. Team members should have opportunities to discuss new insights with each other. They should be challenged to draw implications from the learning experiences that are unique and helpful to them and their congregation. Critical skills will need to be revisited over and over again. New teams often assume that a skill has been mastered once it has been presented and discussed. This is rarely true. Follow-up presentation and discussion is usually needed. Actual practice in applying the skill, constructive feedback, and yet further opportunities for practice are essential for skill development. The complexity of these skills makes this type of creative redundancy important.

The Skills of Team Learning

Just as creative tension leads to individual learning, building a shared vision is a critical step to enable team learning. Unless the group of individuals has a shared commitment to the performance challenge, the urgency for creating a team will be diminished. Team learning also makes active use of the skills associated with mental models. Beyond these, team learning requires close and transparent relationships. It requires an accepted and challenging goal. And it requires a collaborative approach for sharing and examining information. We refer to these three essential team learning skills as *team building, establishing performance challenges,* and *dialogue.*

Team Building

Highly effective teams don't happen overnight or coincidentally. The best teams, whether in a church, sport, or business, combine and leverage many different talents and perspectives. Teams often fail to coalesce because of the challenges in developing close interpersonal relationships. Differences between team members often cause friction and disagreement. Every person brings their own blind spots, hot buttons, and biases. The closer we live and work together the more likely we are to see and experience each other's imperfections.

In an effective team, differences create synergy. Rather than staying a safe distance apart, the close working relationships within a team turn diversity into a source of strength. This does not happen without hard work, but it is achievable. Team building is the place to begin to embrace the differences that the team members bring. The most important steps that change leaders can take to build teams are discussed below.

Establish Values to Guide Team Interactions

Before a team is launched, ground rules need to be established. Team members bring many unexpressed assumptions about what is and is not acceptable in group interaction. For instance, if the pastor expresses an opinion, is it acceptable for a team member to disagree? Should the team use a "majority rules" approach to important decisions? Openness, consensus, mutual respect, creativity, and diversity are some of the typical values of effective teams. For many congregations, however, these values are quite different from the unstated norms.

In Holy Redeemer Church, the pastor emphasized his desire for contrary points of view to be expressed. Yet he often had an intuitive sense that when Marge Lansing disagreed with him, she would hold back. One day in a heated conversation, Marge timidly mustered the courage to express a view that was different from the pastor's. When the meeting was over, he went to Marge and gently said, "Thanks. I know it took a lot of courage for you to disagree with me tonight. I appreciate it. You helped me see something I had not seen before." In that brief interchange, this leader reinforced a value that would foster team learning.

The illustration reflects the importance of declaring a value and enforcing it repeatedly. Mastering team learning will be difficult if values are not made explicit. It will be impossible if they are made explicit but not honored by the change leaders.

Another value to establish is the team's *boundary conditions*. These define the outer limits of acceptability for new ideas. Boundaries can be narrow or wide. For example, are the available options limited to those endorsed by the national denomination? In some congregations, an underlying value is that only denominational programs and priorities can be considered. This and other similar boundaries should be exposed and discussed by the group. Doing so will help establish the team's values and can save a lot of heartache down the road.

Appreciate Differences in Gifts and Styles

Shared experiences should be created to help the team learn to value the different abilities that each member brings. This is done informally as the team spends time together. For team learning to be mastered, however, this experience must also be planned. An annual retreat that focuses on team building is an ideal way to do this. The format should allow time to reinforce the team concept, study the Scriptures, play, rest, and just be together. A retreat that focuses on planning or problem solving will not accomplish this important step.

A team's understanding and appreciation of differences can be enhanced through the use of formal tools like the DISC Personality Profile, Bi/Polar, or Myers-Briggs. These learning-style assessment instruments, especially when used during a retreat or other extended time together, allow the team to develop new insights about each member's contributions. They provide an excellent avenue for affirming each person and for helping all see that they need the strengths of the others to do their best work. We have found that teams bond at a deeper level through these experiences and that building trust is accelerated significantly.

Practice Good Communication Skills

Basic communication skills that are commonly understood and accepted elsewhere are often not practiced in congregations. The use of good communication builds teams and reinforces trust, but failure to do so can undermine the team dynamic. Three specific practices that should be employed are as follows:

- Use "I" language when speaking to the group. "I feel that we should do this," rather than "You just don't understand what I think."

- Clarify before disagreeing. When you think you have a different point of view, first make sure that you know what was meant. "Let me be sure I understand you. It's your sense that. . . ."

- Keep an even tone in your voice. Passion is not a bad thing, but when team relationships are still being formed, passion is often mistaken for anger.

Identify and Address Defensive Routines

Senge (1990) draws from Chris Argyris when he describes defensive routines as "habitual ways of interacting that protect us and others from threat or embarrassment, but which also prevent us from learning" (p. 237). The very definition underscores the fact that teams need a high level of trust and a commitment to a shared vision. Individuals who share a passion for reaching a clearly identified goal might risk threat or embarrassment *if* the risk could significantly advance their cause. Both the perceived gains (progress toward the goal) and the perceived risks (retribution from team members) affect a person's tendency to use defensive routines.

Defensive routines keep the team from fully and openly exploring an issue. In our work with congregations, we have seen many variations. Four of the most common ones are

1. The logical put-down—a strongly analytical person implies that everyone would see it her way if they would just think clearly and logically.

2. Passionate discourse—a persuader uses force of personality and persistence to convince the group to accept his point.

3. Peace-keeping—a conflict avoider tries to keep the group from expressing honest (and sometimes passionate) differences of opinion. Often this person expresses her opinions later in private conversations.

4. Hurt feelings—a silent person refuses to acknowledge his hurt feelings, but then disengages from the dialogue.

Defensive routines undermine the team's ability to learn in subtle but powerful ways. Effective change leaders work with the team to identify defensive routines. They seek to change counterproductive behavior before the team's initial progress and enthusiasm are destroyed. They model the desired behavior and keep the dialogue alive when others try to curtail it.

As people work together, they learn to recognize the defensive routines of others. It is more difficult to see our own defensive routines. "The hardest thing for me to see is me!" Effective teams establish ways to give and receive feedback so that the members become more aware of their own defensive routines.

Pastor Tim Copeland is a classic persuader. His most common defensive routine is passionate discourse. He recounts a powerful but painful learning experience that occurred in a staff meeting. A staff member who reported to Tim had a very different point of view on an important decision. She expressed her opinion, and he attempted to per-suade her that she was wrong. When she held her ground, his persua-sive efforts intensified. Finally (and courageously) she said, "Tim, I see it differently and no amount of persuasion is going to change my per-spective. If you want me to comply—I'll do that. But I don't agree with you on this decision."

This confrontation embarrassed Tim. He explained this to the team and asked for time to reflect before continuing the conversation. A week later, Tim and the rest of the staff returned to the decision, this time using the skill of dialogue. Their final decision was different than either one had advocated.

This event occurred after the staff been working together for more than two years to create a high-performance team. Trust was high and they already had experienced success as a team. Their experience demonstrates that defensive routines are operative even when people have the very best intentions. It also shows that removing them takes courage, discipline, and commitment. The staff's ultimate decision demonstrates what Steven Covey (1989) calls the "third alternative." Getting there is hard work. It is not the quickest way to arrive at an answer, but it is ultimately much more effective for the change leader who wants a committed team rather than a compliant working group.

Team building is not the sole responsibility of the change leader. Individuals contribute to team building by spending time with other members. They should give special attention to the person whose style is their polar opposite. These are the people who are the most difficult to value genuinely. Team members should also reflect on their own per-sonal wiring, affirming their own strengths and being open about their specific challenges. As relationships and trust grow, team members should ask for feedback on their communication skills. The change leader may put the wheels in motion, but high performance teams emerge only when each member actively contributes.

Establishing Performance Challenges

Team learning is more likely to flourish when the group has established clear performance standards for the change process. What needs to be accomplished and in what time frame? Just as creative tension fosters gen-erative learning, setting performance standards promotes team learning. Teams, and change efforts in general, encounter difficulties especially when change leaders "fail to establish clear and meaningful performance demands to which they hold the organization and, most important, themselves accountable" (Katzenbach and Smith, 1993, p. 24).

Establishing performance standards is almost a universal weakness of congregations. Most have chosen to measure only a few basic statistics, such as attendance and finances. These measures are important, but they are not enough. Congregations that identify a shared vision and then establish corresponding standards create a dynamic for learning that is potent. Establishing these standards requires guidance from the change leader and active collaboration by the entire team. If the pastor or a team leader establishes the standards without the team's involvement, the most likely response will be compliance rather than commitment.

The Fellowship of Lockwood addressed this challenge. The vision community was unsure how to set performance standards for "making disciples," which was the focus of the congregation's recently adopted vision statement:

We exist to make as many disciples for Christ as possible using the most effective means available. Making disciples means winning the lost to Christ; baptizing new believers and assimilating them into the local church; teaching, training, nurturing, and equipping all believers for personal growth and for ministry; and sending out believers to be reproducers in the world.

Previously the church had measured attendance at discipleship-training courses and events, but had not tried to assess whether these programs were fulfilling their intended purposes. After several dialogue sessions, the vision community identified seven characteristics that they considered to be indicators of a mature disciple. These included behavior regarding (1) corporate worship, (2) personal daily worship, (3) financial stewardship, (4) service in a specific ministry, (5) involvement in a small group, (6) relationships with unchurched persons, and (7) daily prayer life. The vision community then developed and conducted a survey to ascertain baseline measures for each characteristic. The survey was administered again every six months to evaluate progress. The surveys kept the vision community focused on their goal of making disciples and provided valuable information as they faced decisions of how to pursue God's vision.

Establishing performance standards in a collaborative effort is best done in the context of trusting relationships. Once the standards are set, the team will recognize that it needs to know much more in order to meet the challenge. That is where the third skill, dialogue, becomes a powerful tool for team learning.

Dialogue

"The purpose of dialogue is to go beyond any one individual's under-standing" (Senge, 1990, p. 241). In dialogue, each individual's understand-ing is made available to the entire group so that all learn. Dialogue is distinct from discussion. In *discussion*, an individual's perspective on an issue is presented with the objective of persuading the rest of the group. Discussion, by this definition, often makes group members pro-tective of their turf and can lead to defensiveness (see defensive rou-tines, listed earlier).

In *dialogue*, an individual offers his or her perspective or assump-tions for examination by the group. The object of dialogue is to allow others to see what you see and why you see it, not to convince them. Dialogue can create a rich understanding if information is shared open-ly and if all participants listen deeply.

This can only be done in a safe environment—the type that is estab-lished by team learning. If members of the group expect their views to be disregarded or used against them, dialogue will not occur. Defenses will go up or information will not be fully shared. Senge (1990) identi-fies three key practices for teams engaging the practice of dialogue.

Participants Agree to Describe Their Assumptions

In any conversation, we have many unexpressed assumptions. Often we think that our team shares the same assumptions. At other times we do not want to admit them, and sometimes we are not even aware of what we have assumed. For instance, one person might reject a possible change in the congregation's worship schedule because she knows that conflict will result. She assumes that conflict is not acceptable in the church, so she argues against the schedule change. She might offer a variety of reasons, none having to do with the potential for conflict. In dialogue, as this person recognizes her reasoning, she would make the assumption explicit so that the group could reflect on it and determine whether they share the assumption.

True dialogue allows team members to examine one another's assumptions. As this unfolds, participants often develop new insights into the personal assumptions that they bring to the process. When individuals are defending an opinion, they are unlikely to expose their assumptions. The process of examining our own assumptions and of being open to questioning from others is a challenge for any team.

Participants Agree to Treat One Another as Colleagues

Every member of a group brings expectations regarding an implicit or explicit hierarchy. Hierarchy implies that one team member has a bigger vote or a more important opinion, which in turn hinders dialogue. Consciously setting aside the implications of hierarchies in a congregation is a significant challenge. But Senge (1990) observes that "dialogue can occur only when a group of people see each other as colleagues in mutual quest for deeper insight and clarity" (p. 245).

Hierarchies are not just about organizational or positional power. A group may defer to the person who has more tenure, thinks quicker on his or her feet, or is perceived as the expert in a given area. To master team learning, change leaders must create an environment in which every person, regardless of their position, feels free to contribute.

Viewing one another as colleagues does not mean that individuals must always agree or ultimately share the same view. On the contrary, this practice serves teams most powerfully when individuals hold differing points of view. Of course, it is not easy to forget existing supervisor-subordinate relationships when disagreements arise.

The staff had been discussing a potential reorganization that was particularly complex. In their Monday afternoon team meeting, they had explored several options in detail. Overnight, the team leader had a new thought that had the potential to take the team in an entirely new direction. She immediately shared her thoughts with the entire team by e-mail.

As one of the team members read the note the next day, his immediate thought was, "What is she trying to do to us? This is not what we agreed to yesterday. This makes me so angry." Then he had a breakthrough. He asked himself, "Do I really believe that the team leader is attempting to undermine our process or do I believe that she is deeply committed to our vision and shares our values?" The answers were clear. He realized that they were both attempting to achieve the same results. Afterward he reread the message to see what might be gained from these new thoughts.

Of particular significance in this incident, the team leader was also the other team member's supervisor. Had he not viewed her as a colleague, the process might have had a very different outcome. He might have complained to others on the team, or repressed his anger and focused on how to please his boss. Instead, he treated her like a trusted friend and colleague, and the entire organization benefited from the ensuing dialogue.

A Facilitator Holds Group Members to Their Commitment to Dialogue

Though there are appropriate times for discussion, most groups overuse it. Changing this tendency is hard; it requires commitment, practice, and assistance. A facilitator can strengthen the group members' ability to use dialogue by helping them establish ground rules and calling them back to the rules when they slide from dialogue into discussion. A good facilitator will participate in the dialogue, thereby modeling the behavior that encourages dialogue.

Mastering the skill of dialogue is a painstaking process that typically requires an experienced facilitator when the skill is being learned. Dialogue is risky because it requires a high level of transparency and vulnerability from all participants, especially the team leader. Just as the risks are great, so are the rewards. Dialogue significantly increases a team's ability to achieve the results that God desires.

Conclusion

Change leaders who want to successfully address the challenges of transformation will pay the price to develop effective teams as described in this chapter. In an environment of trusting relationships, team collaboration to set performance standards generates creative tension for the group. Building teams takes time and discipline. The most challenging and potentially most important skill for teams is dialogue. These three skills—team building, performance challenges, and dialogue—will accelerate the entire learning process for a team.

Making the commitment to teams, providing opportunities for skill development, and monitoring the team's progress are crucial roles for change leaders. If congregations are to experience radical transformation, their leadership teams must exhibit sharply increased levels of learning and effectiveness.

Chapter 10

Discipline Four: Practicing Systems Thinking

THOSE OF US who have reared children can tell elaborate stories of parental problem solving. We constantly asked, "What do we do now?" When our baby cried, we grabbed a bottle or a diaper to try to fix her discomfort. When our child was noisy, we attempted to focus his attention on a "calmer" activity. When our teenager was irresponsible, we described the desirable "adult" behavior. In reality, some of our interventions were more appropriate than others. We never completely understood all the underlying factors and whether our action was a help or a hindrance. Along the way, however, we developed certain attitudes and practices—a parenting style.

Congregation leadership is quite similar. We are constantly confronted with situations that seem to cry out, "What should we do now?" We become convinced that a ministry is ineffective so we replace the leaders. When morale is low, we conduct a special spiritual growth "emphasis." Community residents seem reluctant to join our church so we spend money to remodel the facility. These responses seem effective at times and not at others. As we respond, we develop our own approaches to problem solving and our own style of leadership.

How do we determine what is happening in our congregation? What is the basis for our decisions? Some congregational leaders prefer methodical and analytical problem-solving techniques, and others tend to rely on gut-level intuition. Most use a mix of the two. For many years, most formal training and literature has focused on the analytical approach. An organization is dissected into its various components and the problems within a particular part are identified and assessed. Following this approach, the focus of leadership is to analyze the individual parts. A pastor would divide the congregation into its various programs and ministries for evaluation. Worn-out or broken parts (people or programs) are simply replaced with the new and improved models. Sometimes altering a particular cause seems to bring dramatic relief. At other times, we are left wondering why things haven't gotten better after a new solution is implemented. Like the countless hand movements that adjust a car's steering wheel on a long trip, these interventions are incremental shifts in a congregation's way of life.

While small adjustments are necessary, faithful and effective leadership involves much more than merely "tweaking" the organization. A simple cause-and-effect view is too shallow to show the complexities of congregational life. Systems thinking is a far more accurate and useful approach for transformational leaders.

Systems thinking considers interactions between different parts and causes that may not be obvious. It helps integrate the other three learning disciplines—creative tension, mental models, and team learning. The comprehensive and interactive thinking of a systems perspective improves a leader's ability to perceive current reality, discern vision, and improve mental models.

Congregational Systems

The way change leaders view a congregation has a direct bearing on how they assess situations and formulate solutions. Congregations are spiritual and human social systems that are complex, connected, and changing. Each of these characteristics merits closer examination.

Spiritual and Human Social Systems

Like all living entities, congregations require particular resources and conditions in order to thrive. Otherwise they become unhealthy and can even die. Congregations are unique creations of God designed to embody and strengthen our spiritual relationships with Christ and with one another.

God calls each congregation, as a spiritual community, to be faithful and effective. Faithfulness means participating in God's mission to transform all of creation. Effectiveness focuses on stewardship of the resources and opportunities entrusted to the congregation. Trying to be faithful without being effective can lead to withdrawal from the world, or legalism. Trying to be effective without being faithful can lead to worldly kingdom building and meaningless organizational development. Congregations are also human organizations, subject to the same problems and interpersonal dynamics as any other organization. A systems view of a congregation acknowledges the ongoing interaction of its spiritual and material dimensions.

Complex Organizations

Most of us are impressed by the advances of computer technology. However, the most sophisticated computer pales in comparison to the capacities of a human infant. Groups of people are vastly more complex than individuals, and Christian congregations are the most complicated human organizations that exist. Their mix of the human and the divine, a heritage measured in centuries, and variations in size, context, beliefs, values, and practices make them extraordinarily intricate. We are tempted to treat them like social machines by indiscriminately interchanging people, programs, and purposes, but their status as living systems requires a far more nuanced understanding and approach.

Connected Parts and Layers

All parts of the human body are ultimately connected through their interactions and contributions to the entire body's well-being. The external environment also directly affects the body. Consequently, congregations should be viewed as a system of connected internal components that interact with the surrounding environment.

Congregations are *open systems:* everything in them affects everything else. To understand the concept of a system, visualize congregations as comprising four connected "layers." Figure 10.1 depicts these interactive dimensions.

Events

At the surface level are *events,* all of a congregation's routine and special activities. Worship, disciple making, care giving, social gatherings, and community ministries—when looked at independently—are all events. They occur as blocks of time, energy, and activity. This rich and vital layer is where a congregation's mission is lived out. Leaders are constantly drawn to this level, reacting to the constant flow of events with varying amounts of short-term attention. The church benefits (or suffers) immediately based on the outcome of each event.

FIGURE 10.1   Layers of a Congregational System

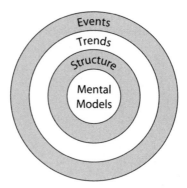

Trends

Trends describe a current direction of a congregation, or of a specific aspect of the congregation, over time. A month-by-month increase in participation in youth events is a trend. Trends may occur over weeks or years. They can be within or beyond the congregation's control. They may include the level of spiritual and relational vitality, the numbers of people in worship or small groups, the effectiveness of ministries, the physical condition of the property, the amount of money contributed, or the composition of surrounding neighborhoods. Trends can involve attitudes, values, or actions.

Leaders should assess whether a trend is desirable, and if not, whether it can be changed. Often leaders respond by altering their attitudes and actions. For example, outreach strategies may be implemented to respond to an attendance decline. Fundraising may be employed when financial contributions are decreasing. Conflict management may be attempted if relationships are deteriorating.

Structure

Structure is the patterns of relationships throughout the congregational system. These interrelated parts include the congregation's history, context, ministries, leadership, identity, and vision. Structure may be expressed through attitudes, actions, values, and beliefs. Structure, as defined here, is not limited to the church's organizational hierarchy, but also includes its predictable ways of thinking and behaving. Structure can be thought of as the way of life that normally functions below the group's conscious awareness. "It's just the way we do things around here."

A congregation's valued traditions operate at the structural level. In one small village congregation, two key families collected and monitored a special designated fund that accumulated over the years. They never reported the value of this fund to the entire congregation because "it would discourage regular giving." The actions of the two families was part of the church's structure, as was the fact that other donors never asked for their gifts to be reported.

Mental Models

Mental models are our perceptions and assumptions concerning the world in which we live (see Chapter Eight). Like structure, we may be conscious of some of our models, but they primarily function below the level of our awareness. Mental models deal with a variety of issues such as the church's mission, the nature of the Gospel, the traits of the people in the community, the exercise of authority, decision making in the congregation, and the role of the church facility.

When a growing ten-year-old congregation sold its original facility and began worshiping in a school, the shift from a "permanent" to a rented space created discomfort for some members about their identity. The leaders realized that a new mental model was required. They began to talk about being in a "Tabernacle" phase moving toward the "Promised Land." The image of being God's people on a pilgrimage served as a powerful new mental model for this congregation.

Events, trends, structures, and mental models are all related. Most of a congregation's perceptions, and most of the leadership's time and energy, are understandably focused on events and trends. But the highest leverage for significant transformation is generally found at the mental model and structural levels.

A new pastor facing a potentially contentious decision is surprised when the congregation quietly defers to his wishes. This single incident is an *event*, but when the same behavior is repeated twice in the next few months it represents a *trend*. As the pastor explores the reasons for the congregation's approach to decision making and conflict, he learns that a split occurred fifteen years earlier. A conflict between the founding pastor and several key lay leaders resulted in the pastor leaving with one-third of the families in the congregation. The *structure* that evolved was one of total submission to the senior pastor's desires. Even though few of the original members were still in the congregation, a *mental model* of conflict-avoidance and pastoral authority deeply influenced each event in the congregation's current life. To enable transformation, change leaders must be able to see and act on each of these four levels.

Constant Change

Some changes are fairly predictable. Like a pendulum, movement in one direction is balanced by movement in the opposite direction. A congregation emphasizes reaching new people and does so effectively. Sensing that the new members are not building meaningful relationships, it embarks on an internal growth emphasis. Shifts of this nature are reversible. They are made to maintain an equilibrium or sense of balance. Congregations make such shifts constantly by doing "more of this and less of that." Gregory Bateson (1979) called this a *first-order change.* In *second-order change,* the consequences are less predictable and are irreversible. Sometimes we initiate them and sometimes they are forced on us. A forest fire illustrates a second-order change. It rages out of control and leaves a radically different environment.

An older leader in an inner-city congregation resisted involvement with poor residents of the community. His focus was on ministries within the walls of the church. Then a friend convinced him to help once in the congregation's food ministry. His service changed his own understanding of the church's mission, and he became a powerful advocate for ministry in the neighborhood. This transformed leader could not return to his previous mental model or way of life.

Congregations need both first- and second-order changes. In first-order changes, incremental and balanced adjustments maintain an essential continuity with the past. They foster a sense of stability. Second-order changes are dramatic shifts that open significant new opportunities and challenges. Afterward, the congregation realizes, "We'll never be the same." When the Hebrews wanted to return to Egypt after experiencing the wilderness, they had a first-order change in mind. But God's plan to lead them to the Promised Land was a radical, second-order transformation.

Components of a Congregational System

What do congregations do? A mental checklist of their components is invaluable before considering the interacting parts and the dynamics of whole churches.

Congregational systems, like human bodies, are made up of many parts. Each contributes to the good of the whole. When the apostle Paul described the church as the body of Christ, he noted that each part had a particular function and that each part needed the others. Unity of the parts stems from the guidance of a common head—Jesus Christ. Paul also described our tendency to discount the importance of some parts at the risk of malfunction and disunity (1 Corinthians 12:21–26; Romans 12:4–5).

Learning how congregations work is not unlike the training of physicians. During their first year of medical school, students learn the complex details of human anatomy and physiology. They must comprehend this information in order to understand their subsequent training on illness and medical intervention. Everything physicians do is based on their knowledge of how the human body is supposed to function.

Likewise, everything church leaders do is shaped by their mental models of how congregations function. Most church leaders focus on certain aspects of the congregation's life, typically the more visible ones, such as worship, Bible study, leadership training, youth ministries, property maintenance, and financial resources. This perspective is not broad enough for pastors and key leaders. An adequately comprehensive view of the congregation as a system ensures that vital components are not overlooked for assessment and attention. Our mental model of a congregation's "bodylife" includes seven major congregational subsystems:

- Mission and Vision
- Boundaries
- Context
- Heritage
- Leadership
- Ministry
- Feedback

Congregational Bodylife

A congregation's *mission and vision* give it purpose and direction. God's reign in our world is established through his ongoing mission, to which congregations are called and empowered to participate. Each congregation moves distinctively toward that mission, as described in its vision. Vision describes specific ways that the congregation will be different a few years in the future. Faithful congregations base their decisions on their missional beliefs and visionary calling.

Congregations have permeable *boundaries*. Physical boundaries identify where they generally gather and serve. Group boundaries describe the identity of each unique body of believers. Group characteristics include demographic factors such as the church's size, the age of its members, and its ethnicity. Other intangible group characteristics include shared values and expectations of the congregation.

Each local body of Christ constantly interacts with many other social entities in its *context*. Context includes the congregation's local community, whether defined by geography or by a particular group of people. The broader social environment or culture around a congregation is another part of its context. Context also reflects religious networks, such as denominational affiliation, interaction with parachurch groups, and alliances with other local churches.

A congregation's *heritage* represents every aspect of its life before the current date. Its spiritual and relational journey is the story of how faithfully the people have followed God and the quality of their relationships with one another. The journey of most congregations includes plenty of high and low points. Heritage also includes organizational history—the influence of people, circumstances, and events in the past that shaped the congregation. Heritage includes the congregation's interaction with its context over time. Churches have a natural tendency to become less involved in their communities as they grow and mature.

Leadership is the subsystem in which spiritual, relational, and organizational change are initiated and guided. Spiritual and relational vitality (see Chapter Two) creates a unified body and establishes the conditions for transformation. The change process, the calling of leaders, and the development of critical learning disciplines are all aspects of transformational leadership. All of these should contribute to the capacity of the entire congregation to function as a learning community.

Ministry is an elaborate subsystem that encompasses all the practices of a congregation as it lives its mission and vision. This includes the implementation of various ministries, like worship, disciple-making, care giving, and social action. It also includes formal organizational structures and formal and informal processes, such as decision making, communication, and delegation of authority and responsibility. A final aspect of ministry mobilization is the congregation's stewardship of God-given resources such as money, skill, and time.

The *feedback* subsystem includes the ways a congregation measures its qualitative and quantitative progress toward God's vision. Feedback is always occurring, but leaders may not interpret or use it appropriately.

Understanding the major elements of congregational life provides a way to inventory the key areas that contribute to overall church health and helps leaders design more effective intervention strategies. Intervention may involve directly addressing the area that seems to be weak, the *presenting problem*. This type of surface approach will not alter the powerful underlying forces that often undermine progress. Deeper and longer-term impact is achieved by changing other areas that are contributing to the presenting problem. Finding and correcting the most significant of these underlying factors is a *high-leverage intervention*. This comprehensive approach to understanding and leading congregations is basic to a systems thinking approach.

For instance, poor teaching may be addressed by providing training in teaching skills. However, the quality of the teaching may be influenced even more by the teachers' unfamiliarity with the needs and concerns of the class or their own inadequate level of discipleship. In those cases, mere teacher training may create more frustration than help because valuable time and energy appear to be wasted.

Sophisticated tools for diagraming these complex interrelationships within a system have been developed by Peter Senge and Daniel Kim of MIT's Center for Organizational Learning (Senge, 1990; Anderson and Johnson, 1997). Patterns of influence among key factors are depicted through what they call "causal loop diagrams." Some generic organizational patterns occur so commonly that they are described as "systems archetypes" (Kim and Anderson, 1998).

Five Whys

The Five Whys technique is a powerful diagnostic skill that helps leaders move from a presenting problem to deeper layers of understanding (Ross, 1994, pp. 108–112). When using the Five Whys approach, leaders identify a presenting problem and then ask, "Why is this happening?" After one list of several factors is generated, they repeat the process, looking for answers that provide deeper explanations for each factor rather than simple blame. After five rounds of "why?" a few issues will generally surface as the primary underlying sources of the problem. Dealing with those factors is a high-leverage strategy for changing the entire system.

Seventh Street Church had been isolated from its neighborhood for many years. Despite tight resources, the pastor insisted that they begin offering General Equivalency Diploma classes and support groups for single mothers in the community. The ministry was always short on workers, and after a year, only a handful of community residents were involved. The morale of the struggling church reached new lows, and the leaders began to consider disbanding. At that point, three of the single moms, who had life-changing experiences in the program, joined the church and volunteered to coordinate the ministry. In a few months, several dozen women from the neighborhood had begun to participate. This experience gave Seventh Street's leaders a deep sense of encouragement and commitment to continue to touch their community.

The Five Whys approach could be applied, starting with the presenting problem: "Why is participation low in Seventh Street's community ministries?" Limited awareness of the services within the community would be the first-level answer. This, in turn, was partially the result of the residents not talking about the program with each other, which stemmed from their mistrust of the church. The lack of trust was caused by Seventh Street's poor reputation after years of low involvement in the community.

Stopping at the first-level why could have led to the wrong conclusion. Extensive publicity in the neighborhood would not have stimulated higher participation, and the failure would have hurt the congregation's morale even more. At Seventh Street, the three new members were able to bridge the gap between the community and the congregation. Their interaction with their neighbors provided a positive awareness and trust that had been missing.

As this analysis shows, a variety of conclusions can be drawn from the same initial set of facts. Congregations need to use systems thinking to identify the high-leverage actions that will generate the greatest benefits.

Dynamic Qualities of Congregational Systems

Understanding a church's bodylife helps change leaders perceive the *substance* of specific relationships among a congregation's components. They also need to understand the general principles of congregations that we refer to as congregational *dynamics*. Seven predictable dynamics of congregational life are summarized in this section. These dynamics are present in every congregation. Change leaders need to accurately assess how these dynamics are affecting their congregations.

Congregations Have Personality

Each congregation is a unique combination of people at a particular place in time. Just as, among the six billion persons inhabiting the planet, no two people are the same, no two congregations are the same. And like all other human groups, congregations develop a self-preserving way of life over time—an organizational culture.

This means that if a congregation is split in half, the two halves will not be the same. More important, programs from other churches cannot be replicated to produce the exact same results every time. Neither will a new pastor or other leader be guaranteed repeat success in a new congregation.

Change leaders should always start with a clear understanding of their congregation, its unique culture, and environment. They should always be open to new ideas but always be wary of a "universal" program that claims to fit any congregation. Recognizing that their congregation has a unique personality, the leaders should pursue God's unique vision for the future of their congregation.

Every Change Changes Everything

A central tenet of systems thinking is that the components of the system are all interrelated. Therefore, a change in one component will ripple through the entire system. Our mental models, however, tend to simplify the system. As a result, leaders routinely underestimate the complexity of congregational life. They want to explain each issue easily and to intervene directly and decisively. In reality, any given issue is influenced by all of the actions, attitudes, decisions, people, and artifacts that constitute the congregation. This interaction takes place regardless of whether it is seen or understood.

The leaders of a sixty-year-old congregation realized that respect for the office of the pastor was low. What was less obvious, however, was the influence of the events that had led to four of the last six pastors being fired. With each new dismissal, the congregation's attitudes about the office and role of the pastor were affected. The trust and respect that might have been expected were replaced with mistrust and criticism. Without being conscious of this dynamic, current church leaders often overreacted to the new pastor's mistakes and even discounted his good faith efforts. The unresolved pain, fear, and anger from these past hurts silently but steadily drained their energy and crippled the congregation's ability to actively pursue God's vision.

The full consequences of a change are often subtle because they may not become evident until a much later date. The impact may have actually worked its way through several other parts of the system first. Change leaders should always look for the broader and unintended impacts of a change. Rather than accepting the simple explanations or pat answers to every problem, they should probe deeper for other contributing factors. If we remember that there is never just one reason for an event, we can begin to perceive the nature of congregational life more accurately and richly.

The Past Is Always Present

Everything that happens in a congregation becomes a permanent part of its identity. Unusually bad episodes and exceptionally outstanding successes are the two most common sources of long-term influence in a congregation. Many congregations have had traumatic experiences in which people were deeply hurt. Dealing with such wounds requires patient and sensitive attention. The consequences of anger, guilt, and abuse do not go away automatically.

On the other hand, past accomplishments can have a positive or negative influence. For some congregations, their successes inspire a can-do attitude toward new challenges. Unfortunately, more congregations try to recreate past successes by repeating the watershed event or program without evaluating its likely outcome in the current context.

Bayside Church's leaders had been talking intently for two hours. The mood was tense. For the third time in six months, a creditor had threatened to sue the church for nonpayment of a long overdue bill. Weekly contributions were not meeting the budget. But the new pastor was astonished to learn that the church had a ten thousand dollar certificate of deposit in the bank. After enough probing and active listening, the story became clear. When the church was young and struggling, a bank almost foreclosed on the its mortgage. Several key members at that time were the current leaders at Bayside. They remembered their promise to never be without cash in the bank, no matter what happened. The commitment made in a previous situation still yielded substantial impact in the present and different circumstance.

Central Church served a neighborhood made up almost entirely of older adults and families with very young children. Even though only three or four teens regularly attended, the congregation had a full-time youth pastor and a generous program budget for youth-related activities. Search committees had called the last two pastors to Central directly from roles as youth ministers, thinking that this would help attract more youth. Neither had the experience or skills to lead a stagnant congregation effectively, and both resigned after short tenures, feeling frustrated and confused. A long-term member explained, "We've been in the church for thirty years. Most of us reared our children here. At one time, kids came to Central from all around because we had the best youth ministry in the city. Those were our best days. We know that a dynamic youth ministry is always the key for a church to be successful."

Congregations need to learn from past successes and failures to stimulate current growth and vitality. Change leaders should be sensitive to attempts to return to the glory days—"The way we did it before." They should also be sensitive to indications of past, unresolved wounds. If these seem to create a significant ongoing drag on the congregation's vitality, the need for public or private reconciliation should be explored. The past can be leveraged as a springboard to the future or it can become a ball and chain that the congregation cannot seem to escape.

Congregations Talk Their Walk

Leaders often feel like they are in the dark about much of what is happening in their congregations. In reality, we frequently overlook or misinterpret streams of information that are readily available. Every action a congregation takes (or doesn't take) can be a source of *feedback* for the change leader. Such information describes where the church is on the journey toward its vision.

Most churches pay attention to just a few vital signs, even though data can be obtained for any aspect of congregational life. Feedback can come from many sources, including direct observation, church records, written surveys, and personal interviews. Feedback can be active (what people say and do) or passive (what people don't say and don't do). Some feedback points to additional information that is needed to better assess an issue.

Good information is a critical building block for transformation. Change leaders should assess the extent and quality of the feedback that they are receiving. Is feedback available for all of the important aspects of the congregation? In what areas is additional information needed? Change leaders also need to evaluate the message in the feedback. Does our walk match our talk; if not, what is this telling us? Are we using feedback to inform and guide our decisions and actions? Whether leaders gain the full benefit of feedback or ignore and distort it, congregations will continue to tell their stories.

Congregations Change in Order to Stay the Same

Congregations naturally alter their behavior to maintain the status quo. We often hear the statement "Congregations resist change." It this true? Yes and no. Like any organization, congregations develop a way of life that enables them to survive. This leads to an "instinctive" drive to "do what we've always done." However, they also have a natural drive to adapt to their circumstances as necessary for survival.

The new Spring Valley Church emphasized close relationships during its first few months. The initial fifty members bonded intimately with one another. This was a strong attraction for other care-craved families in the community. As more and more new people visited and began to participate in the congregation, the founding group had difficulty finding time to spend time with their old friends. They became considerably less open to newcomers, and the church's rate of growth began to decrease. Interestingly, the leaders were not even aware of why their attractiveness was waning. They had, in fact, changed—in order to stay the same.

Our tendency to maintain the status quo provides stability and continuity for the group. The risk is that it can distort God's mandate for personal and corporate transformation. In some circumstances, the refusal to change at deep levels leads to the death of the congregation. Change leaders should recognize both sides of this dynamic. They should continually ask whether they have found the right balance between stability and transformation.

"Solving" a Problem Can Make Things Worse

When a problem arises, most leaders have a strong urge to fix it. One of the paradoxes of systems thinking is that the apparent problem and the real problem may be entirely different, which means that the apparent solution is not necessarily the right one.

The leaders of St. Mark's Church complained that more members needed to assume active roles and share the load of pursuing God's vision. They viewed the lack of involvement as an indicator that others were not really committed to the vision. In response, the active leaders spent all of their time and energy running the key ministries. The harder they worked, the less other members seemed to become involved.

Although the latter group may not have been fully committed to the vision, it was hard for them to believe that their investment was truly needed since everything was being done. In this case, the "solution" of the leaders working harder was exacerbating the problem.

Such self-defeating efforts can become unhealthy addictions. Leaders say they want to break out of their current reality, but they fail to exercise the available options. It can be argued that churches always get what they *really* want. The full consequences of our actions may not be obvious in advance, but systems thinking gives us a tool for understanding the likely outcomes. Change leaders should use caution when applying quick-fix remedies. Whenever possible, they should devote the time to find the *real* solution to their biggest challenges.

Strategic Points of Leverage Exist Within Systems

Leaders often realize that their congregation needs to change but feel like it is stuck in a holding pattern. Regardless of the situation, strategic points of leverage always exist within the congregational system. The fundamental challenge for leaders is to locate and act on these opportunities.

Such high-leverage points are often in places that are counterintuitive, that is, they don't seem obvious or probable. The concepts and approaches discussed in this chapter are the starting point for identifying these hidden alternatives. Change leaders should look at the congregation as a complex, interrelated system. They should probe beyond the surface to understand the real factors that are contributing to a problem. Rather than implementing the obvious answer, they should look for the solution that provides the highest leverage. And mostly, they should never stop learning about the ever-changing system that they are attempting to influence.

In one of our consultations, the pastor moaned, "I don't want to do the systems stuff. It makes my head hurt." It is challenging to treat a congregation as a spiritual and human social system that is complex, connected, and changing. It is also more accurate to do so. The benefits of accurate diagnosis and wise intervention make systems thinking a discipline that is well worth the effort to master.

Chapter 11

The Art of Transformational Leadership

CONGREGATIONAL TRANSFORMATION is a balancing act in many different respects. Change leaders will be pulled between the daily demands of managing the congregation's routine activities and the need to devote considerable time to the long-term change process. Change itself needs to be balanced between leading the congregation forward and pausing to allow members to catch their breath. The model for transformation described in this book involves a balance among making progress on the change process, fostering spiritual and relational vitality, and mastering the learning disciplines.

Many similarities can be found between the transformational leader and a high-wire performer. Life on the high wire demands constant balance. It has certain and significant risks and rewards. We could describe the performance using the laws of physics—gravitational forces, center of gravity, and force diagrams. But what we observe is more artistry than science. We would not think of attempting their daring feats, but the truth is that they are human beings just like us. They started at the simplest and lowest level, and developed their skill with much practice and coaching.

Being a transformational leader is equal parts science and art. It requires continuous learning and skill development. It helps immensely to have wise mentors. We may see great leaders and wonder how they do it, but the truth is that God has placed tremendous capability in each of us. And it is a calling that is full of risks and rewards.

At the conclusion of our congregational transformation seminars, we know to expect one recurring question: "There is so much to learn. Where do I begin?" We do not disagree with this assessment, but we encourage participants not to become discouraged. It is not necessary to learn everything at once. The best course is to begin mastering the material that is appropriate for your particular situation and to continue to grow in your ability to be an effective change leader.

Realities of Transformational Dynamics

It is also helpful for a change leader to hold a clear mental model of the nature of transformation. Even though each congregation—and therefore each transformational journey—is unique, certain aspects of transformation are so predictable that they can be described as "universal." These six dynamics summarize our perspective on congregational transformation.

Spiritual and Relational Vitality Drives Transformation

Leaders have an array of options available to motivate people. In the short term, fear, guilt, persuasion, manipulation, coercion, or even bribery might stimulate action. Ultimately, long-term transformation is only possible when a congregation faithfully and corporately pursues God's will for its future. Not only is this energy the power behind redemptive change, it is the way of life intended by God for obedient disciples. Spiritual and relational vitality means doing what we should do because of who we are in Christ. At a given point in time, many aspects of congregational life may need to be altered. The primary motivation to deal with such issues should flow from God's transforming vitality in the fellowship of a Christian community.

Congregational Transformation Requires Transformed Leaders

Congregations are different from business organizations. Paid church leaders should not fall into the trap of acting like detached professionals. The spiritual health of the pastor and other key leaders is intimately intertwined with that of the congregation. A congregation will rarely grow beyond the health of its pastor and key leaders. The first step of the transformational journey is the leaders' own self-examination and willingness to be personally transformed.

Transformation Occurs Through Intentional Processes

Change is difficult to initiate. Effective congregational change requires someone to lead it toward a common destination. For some leaders, initiating and guiding change is an intuitive ability. But even the most gift-ed natural leader needs to follow an intentional process. The eight stages of the change process provide direction and order, even in the midst of complicated situations. The interaction between the change process and the other aspects of transformation—spiritual and relational vitality and learning disciplines—should also reflect intentional design.

Each Transformation Process Is Unique

Every congregation is a distinct and complex entity. Each church develops a certain style, has a particular history, comprises a unique collection of individuals, and serves in a specific context. No two congregations are alike. Consequently, the journey to a new future must be customized for those people in that time and place. Principles may be readily transferred, but prescriptions need to be carefully tailored.

Congregational Transformation Requires Specific Skills

A congregation rarely has leaders who naturally possess all the abilities needed to move through the change process. The disciplines described in Chapters Seven through Ten are needed in each step of transformation. Change leaders should plan on investing time in personal and congregational learning. They should also continuously look for individuals who possess specific needed skills.

Even Healthy Change Takes Time

Congregational change is normally slow if the changes are appropriately deep and wide. Deep changes are those that move beyond superficial circumstances, such as attendance and morale, to the underlying corporate attitudes and practices, such as the structures and mental models of the congregation. Changes are wide if they are comprehensive. For a congregation to experience deep and lasting change, all of its major parts must be moving in the same direction. When significant aspects of its bodylife are incongruent with the vision, vital energy is lost and confusion is generated. Congregations in which the bodylife subsystems are aligned have tremendous power. Creating alignment among the parts takes time, but it leads to a rich blessing.

Challenges of Transformational Leadership

Leadership is always challenging. Congregational life further compounds the generic demands of leadership in three ways. First, leaders are not really in charge. Church leaders are followers of the living God who directs their lives through the Holy Spirit. They are, however, called to initiate transformation in the corporate life of the congregation where they serve. A natural tension exists in this dichotomy. Some leaders are inclined to relieve this tension by becoming passive figureheads who affirm God's activity but avoid all risks in their role. Others tend to become aggressive change agents, deferring to God only for a rubber-stamp approval of their own decisions. Transformational leadership calls for *responsive initiative.*

Second, leadership requires enormous personal maturity and assurance in who God created us to be. A group of any size makes many demands that create great pressure for its leaders. Again, opposing forces are at work. Leaders can take a laissez faire approach and allow the diverse wishes of the group to provide the direction and impetus for the body. Or they can minimize distractions from the participants by becoming dictatorial. Either way, any anxieties that they have about themselves as individuals serve as "hooks" for parishioners to grab. This dynamic can instigate a reactive lifestyle that torments and cripples unhealthy leaders. Transformational leadership involves *nonanxious assertiveness.*

Third, leadership can never be fully mastered. Human and congregational dynamics are incredibly complex. In the face of this, it is tempting to choose one portion of the congregation that appears to be controllable and focus on managing it well. But the systems nature of congregational life demands comprehensive and ongoing attention. The transformation process described in this book cannot be used as a neat formula. Its parts and processes will unfold differently in every application. Leadership is more art than science. It requires sound thinking, sensitive feelings, and profound spirituality. Leaders find ways to increase their capacities in every successful and disappointing experience. Transformational leaders practice *masterful learning.*

Conclusion

We began this chapter discussing the multiple balancing challenges that confront change leaders. We also faced a balancing challenge in writing this book. We hope that we have found an appropriate balance in describing the risks and rewards of congregational transformation. We do not want to suggest that a change leader will find the path to be easy. But neither do we want to suggest that the journey is not worth taking.

We find the contemporary words of Bill Hybels to be helpful in reminding us of the ultimate impact that transformed churches can have (Hybels and Hybels, 1995, p. 163):

You tell me: what is nobler, what is loftier, what is a higher purpose in life, than devoting yourself to establishing and developing a community of believers that strives to fulfill the Acts 2 description of the bride of Christ? To creating a supportive and encouraging place where Spirit-led preaching brings a new, God-focused direction to people's lives; where believers gather in small groups to share their hearts on the deepest levels; where people compassionately walk with each other through life's problems and pain; where everyone feels empowered to make a difference through their spiritual gifts; where prayer, worship, and the sacraments are lifted up; where the rich share their God-given resources with the poor; and where people ache so much for their irreligious friends that the church gets strategic and takes risks to reach out to them with the Gospel?

Our hope and prayer is that each person who reads this book will become a more faithful and effective change leader, and that an increasing number of congregations will be transformed through the power of God to reach our world.

Resource

An Annotated Bibliography of Useful Publications

Ammerman, N. T., Carroll, J. W., Dudley, C. S., and McKinney, W. (eds.). *Studying Congregations: A New Handbook.* Nashville, Tenn.: Abingdon Press, 1998.
   A scholarly but accessible guide to conducting a comprehensive congregational study.

Bandy, T. G. *Moving off the Map: A Field Guide to Changing the Congregation.* Nashville, Tenn.: Abingdon Press, 1998.
   Describes an insightful process by which church leaders can better understand their current situation and move toward God's vision for them.

Blackaby, H. T., and King, C. V. *Experiencing God.* Nashville, Tenn.: Broadman and Holman, 1990.
   Uses a workbook format to help readers explore the depth of their willingness and calling to participate in God's movement in our world.

Cladis, G. *Leading the Team-Based Church: How Pastors and Church Staffs Can Grow Together into a Powerful Fellowship of Leaders.* San Francisco: Jossey-Bass, 1999.
   A theologically grounded resource of practical strategies for helping groups become genuine teams.

Clapp, R. *A Peculiar People: The Church as Culture in a Post-Christian Society.* Downers Grove, Ill.: InterVarsity Press, 1996.
   An extremely challenging call to practice Christian community in a powerful and prophetic manner.

Collins, J. C., and Porras, J. I. *Built to Last: Successful Habits of Visionary Companies.* New York: HarperBusiness, 1994.
  Based on an exhaustive study of dozens of companies with long histories of success, the authors summarize the keys to organizations with enduring legacies.

Dennison, J. *City Reaching: On the Road to Community Transformation.* Pasadena, Calif.: William Carey Library, 1999.
  The transformation of individual congregations may well converge with this powerful new movement that mobilizes "the whole church to reach a whole city with the whole gospel."

Hawkins, T. R. *The Learning Congregation: A New Vision of Leadership.* Louisville, Ky.: Westminster/John Knox, 1997.
  An overview of how the concepts of learning organizations apply to congregations.

Hunsberger, G. R., and Van Gelder, C. (eds.). *The Church Between Gospel and Culture: The Emerging Mission in North America.* Grand Rapids, Mich.: Eerdmans, 1996.
  A rich volume summoning the church in North America to abandon its historic coziness with culture and assert its distinctive missional character in our postmodern context.

Katzenbach, J. R., and Smith, D. K. *The Wisdom of Teams: Creating the High-Performance Organization.* Boston: Harvard Business School Press, 1993.
  A classic treatment of the nature of high-performance teams and what it takes to become one.

Morris, D. E., and Olsen, C. M. *Discerning God's Will Together: A Spiritual Practice for the Church.* Nashville, Tenn.: Upper Room, 1997.
  A guide for vision discernment that takes seriously the spiritual nature of the process.

Parsons, G., and Leas, S. B. *Understanding Your Congregation as a System: The Manual.* Bethesda, Md.: Alban Institute, 1993.
  The authors provide a very useful approach to assessing and addressing seven of the most crucial systems of congregational life.

The self-scoring inventories include basic interpretations; the manual explains the dynamics in more detail.

Quinn, R. E. *Deep Change: Discovering the Leader Within.* San Francisco: Jossey-Bass, 1996.
Challenges readers to embrace the necessary but most difficult aspect of leadership—personal transformation.

Rendle, G. R. *Leading Change in the Congregation: Spiritual and Organizational Tools for Leaders.* Bethesda, Md.: Alban Institute, 1998.
A pithy guide that offers lots of helpful tools for understanding and implementing change from an organizational systems perspective.

Schaller, L. E. *The Interventionist.* Nashville, Tenn.: Abingdon Press, 1997.
An exhaustive set of church diagnostic frameworks and questions from one of the most recognized veterans of church consulting.

Senge, P. M. *The Fifth Discipline: The Art and Practice of the Learning Organization.* New York: Doubleday, 1990.
The seminal publication that inaugurated a new level of emphasis on organizations of all types as learning organizations.

Senge, P. M., and others. *The Fifth Discipline Fieldbook: Strategies and Tools for Building a Learning Organization.* New York: Doubleday, 1994.
A virtual encyclopedia of insights and techniques for mastering the disciplines of the learning organization.

Shawchuck, N., and Heuser, R. *Managing the Congregation: Building Effective Systems to Serve People.* Nashville, Tenn.: Abingdon Press, 1996.
A comprehensive overview of how church leaders can use a systems approach to align their congregation in ways that achieve shared vision.

Steinke, P. L. *Healthy Congregations.* Bethesda, Md.: Alban Institute, 1996.
Applies the insights of family systems theory to congregational life, offering useful concepts and skills.

Warren, R. *The Purpose Driven Church*. Grand Rapids, Mich.: Zondervan, 1995.

An extremely readable volume about how Saddleback Church in California developed. Warren describes the power of a church that is highly aligned from purpose to parking lots.

Willard, D. *The Divine Conspiracy: Rediscovering Our Hidden Life in God*. New York: HarperCollins, 1998.

A profound work about living as a faithful disciple.

References

Aldrich, J. *Reunitus: Building Bridges to Each Other Through Prayer Summits.* Sisters, Oreg.: Questar, 1994.

Anderson, V., and Johnson, L. *Systems Thinking Basics: From Concepts to Causal Loops.* Cambridge, Mass.: Pegasus, 1997.

Barker, J. A. *Future Edge: Discovering the New Paradigms of Success.* New York: Morrow, 1992.

Barna, G. *The Second Coming of the Church.* Nashville, Tenn.: Word, 1998.

Bass, B. *Leadership and Performance Beyond Expectations.* New York: Free Press, 1985.

Bateson, G. *Mind and Nature: A Necessary Unity.* New York: Dutton, 1979.

Bennis, W., and Nanus, B. *Leaders: The Strategies for Taking Charge.* New York: HarperCollins, 1985.

Blackaby, H. T., and King, C. V. *Experiencing God: Knowing and Doing the Will of God.* Nashville, Tenn.: Broadman and Holman, 1990.

Blanchard, K. H. "Situational Self-Leadership: Taking the Lead When You're Not in Charge." Escondido, Calif.: Blanchard Training and Development, 1992.

Bunker, B. B., and Alban, B. T. *Large Group Interventions: Engaging the Whole System for Rapid Change.* San Francisco: Jossey-Bass, 1997.

Burns, J. M. *Leadership.* New York: HarperCollins, 1978.

Collins, J. C., and Porras, J. I. *Built to Last: Successful Habits of Visionary Companies.* New York: HarperBusiness, 1994.

Covey, S. A. *The Seven Habits of Highly Effective People: Powerful Lessons in Personal Change.* New York: Simon & Schuster, 1989.

Foster, R. J. *Celebration of Discipline: The Path to Spiritual Growth.* (rev. ed.) New York: HarperCollins, 1988.

Hybels, L., and Hybels, B. *Rediscovering Church: The Story and Vision of Willow Creek Community Church.* Grand Rapids, Mich.: Zondervan, 1995.

Katzenbach, J. R., and Smith, D. K. *The Wisdom of Teams: Creating the High-Performance Organization.* Boston: Harvard Business School Press, 1993.

Kim, D. H., and Anderson, V. *Systems Archetype Basics: From Story to Structure.* Cambridge, Mass.: Pegasus, 1998.

Kotter, J. P. *Leading Change.* Boston: Harvard Business School Press, 1996.

Kuhn, T. *The Structure of Scientific Revolutions.* (2nd ed.) Chicago: University of Chicago Press, 1970.

Leas, S. B. *Discover Your Conflict Management Style.* (rev. ed.) Bethesda, Md.: Alban Institute, 1997.

Lewis, P. V. *Transformational Leadership: A New Model for Total Church Involvement.* Nashville, Tenn.: Broadman and Holman, 1996.

Maxwell, J. C. *The Success Journey: The Process of Living Your Dreams.* Nashville, Tenn.: Nelson, 1997.

Mintzberg, H. *The Rise and Fall of Strategic Planning: Reconceiving Roles for Planning, Plans, and Planners.* New York: Free Press, 1994.

Quinn, R. E. *Deep Change: Discovering the Leader Within.* San Francisco, Calif.: Jossey-Bass, 1996.

Ross, R. "The Five Whys." In P. M. Senge and others, *The Fifth Discipline Fieldbook: Strategies and Tools for Build a Learning Organization.* New York: Doubleday, 1994.

Schaller, L. E. *The Interventionist.* Nashville, Tenn.: Abingdon Press, 1997.

Senge, P. M. *The Fifth Discipline: The Art and Practice of the Learning Organization.* New York: Doubleday, 1990.

Tichy, N. M., and Devanna, M. A. *The Transformational Leader: The Key to Global Competitiveness.* New York: Wiley, 1986.

Warren, R. *The Purpose Driven Church.* Grand Rapids, Mich.: Zondervan, 1995.

The Authors

Jim Herrington is the executive director of Mission Houston, a interdenominational, multicultural group of churches cooperating to complete the Great Commission beginning in the Greater Houston, Texas, area. He earned a B.S. degree (1977) in psychology at the University of Arkansas, Fayetteville, and an M.A. degree in religious education from Southwestern Baptist Theological Seminary in Fort Worth, Texas. Before joining Mission Houston, he served for ten years as the executive director of Union Baptist Association, an association of approximately five hundred churches in the Houston area.

Herrington specializes in pastoral leadership development and leading congregational change. He has consulted with more than one hundred congregations and denominational entities in the areas of congregational transformation, conflict management, leadership development, and spiritual vitality. He is a regular presenter at the Purpose Driven Church seminar on the topic of change leadership.

Mike Bonem is president of Kingdom Transformation Partners, an organization that provides consulting and training assistance to local congregations and denominational entities. He obtained his M.B.A. degree, with distinction, from Harvard Business School in 1985, after having obtained a B.S. degree in chemical engineering from Rice University in 1981.

Bonem's activities have included business consulting with McKinsey and Company and SRI Consulting and congregational consulting with Union Baptist Association in Houston, Texas. His consulting emphasizes strategy and change leadership, particularly in established organizations.

His work with local churches focuses on facilitation of the change process, congregational assessments, vision discernment, and implementation planning. He advocates the adaptation of leading business principles for application by churches. He has also developed and taught seminars on leading congregational change.

Bonem is an active member of a local church and has served as a deacon and a volunteer leader in various aspects of congregational life, including Bible study, finance, human resources, and planning.

James H. Furr is a senior church consultant with Union Baptist Association (UBA) in Houston, Texas; adjunct professor of sociology at Houston Baptist University; and founder of FaithSystems. He earned his B.A. degree (1977) in telecommunications at Texas Tech University in Lubbock; his M.Div. degree (1980) in biblical studies at Midwestern Baptist Theological Seminary in Kansas City, Missouri; and his Ph.D. degree (1987) in church and community studies at Southern Baptist Theological Seminary in Louisville, Kentucky. Prior to his ten years with UBA, he served with Long Run Baptist Association in Louisville for six years and as pastor and church staff person of congregations in Missouri, Kentucky, and Texas.

Furr's major areas of consulting and training include church and community assessment, congregational transformation processes, pastoral leadership development, church conflict management, Christian social ministries, and church consultant development. He is a member of the Religious Research Association and the evangelical Council on Ecclesiology and a participant in the Gospel and Our Culture Network.

To Contact the Authors

To reach the authors for questions or to inquire about support for congregational transformation initiatives:

Mike Bonem or Jim Herrington
Kingdom Transformation Partners
P.O. Box 2272
Bellaire, TX 77402
kingdom-transformation@worldnet.att.net
Phone: (713) 838-9476

Kingdom Transformation Partners provides consulting and training services for individual congregations, denominations, and other Christian organizations. Consulting projects are typically customized to fit the specific needs of the congregation. Other services include teaching seminars on congregational change, leading retreats, supporting denominational or judicatory transformation initiatives, speaking at conferences, and training pastors and other congregational leaders.

Dr. James H. Furr
FaithSystems
9634 S. Kensington Drive
Houston, TX 77031
Phone: (281) 568-3303
E-mail: Furr@faithsystems.com
Website: www.faithsystems.com
FaithSystems provides training and consulting services for congregations, church leaders, and faith-based organizations. Training and presentation topics include change leadership skills, dealing with resistance to change, understanding how your church and community really work, the habits of healthy churches, and living God's vision. Consulting services range from short-term assessments to long-term transformation processes.

About Leadership Network

The mission of Leadership Network is to accelerate the emergence of effective churches by identifying and connecting innovative church leaders; providing them with resources in the form of new ideas, people, and tools; and communicating its learnings to the broader church. Churches and church leaders served by Leadership Network represent a wide variety of primarily Protestant faith traditions that range from mainline to evangelical to independent. They are characterized by innovation, entrepreneurial leadership, and a desire to be on the cutting edge of ministry.

Leadership Network's focus has been on the practice and application of faith at the local congregational level. A sister organization, the Leadership Training Network, uses peer learning and interactive training to accelerate the lay mobilization movement and gift-based team ministry.

Established as a private foundation in 1984 by social entrepreneur Bob Buford, Leadership Network is acknowledged as an influential leader among churches and parachurch ministries and a major resource to which innovative church leaders turn for networking and information.

For additional information contact Leadership Network directly:

Leadership Network
2501 Cedar Springs, Suite 200
Dallas, TX 75201
Phone: (800) 765-5323
Fax: (214) 969-9392
E-mail: info@leadnet.org
Internet: www.leadnet.org

Index

A

Accountability: performance standards and, 139; team learning and, 98, 131, 139; in teams versus working groups, 131; of transformational leaders, 32, 75, 98

Acknowledgment of reality, 106–107. *See also* Current reality

Action plans: development and implementation of, 78, 79, 81–82, 84–85; identifying and implementing new, 89

Acts, 35; 1:6, 114; 2, 17, 18; 2:43,47b, 16; 6, 9; 6:1-6, 19; 11:1-18, 19

Alban, B. T., 54

Aldrich, J., 17

Alignment, 5, 70, 85–94; aspects of, 87; benefits of, 93; of existing ministries with vision, 89–90; of gifts with needs, 83; with God, 20; interdependencies and, 123; key challenge in, 94; reinforcing momentum through (stage 8 of change process), 70, 85–94; suggested actions for, 88–93. *See also* Commitment

Alternate scenarios, 124

American culture: learning in, 129; role of the church in, 115–117

Ammerman, N. T., 163

Amos, 4:13, 17

Analogies for vision, 66

Anderson, V., 151

Apathy, 103

Apollos, 128–129

Apostles' Creed, 35

Apprenticeship, leadership, 74

Argyris, C., 136–137

Assessment: analytical versus systems approach to, 143–144; of conflict management styles, 46, 110; congregational, 39, 155–156; of current reality, 37–41; of current structures and procedures, 75–76; of external and internal measures, 6; of mental models, 117–122; of personality and learning styles, 136; self, of transformational leaders, 31–32, 106, 111, 117–118, 159; of spiritual and relational vitality, 10. *See also* Measurement

Assumptions: identification of, 123, 140–141; team dialogue and, 140–141. *See also* Mental models

Attendance decline, critical thinking about, 121–122

Attendance measurement, 83

Authentic transparency, 117–118

Avoiding style, 110, 111, 137, 147–148